Book 1

A 90-Day Devotional

By Samantha Hanni

BLOOM BOOK 1
2018 Second Edition
Printed by CreateSpace
ISBN-13: 978-1539501411
ISBN-10: 1539501418

Table of Contents

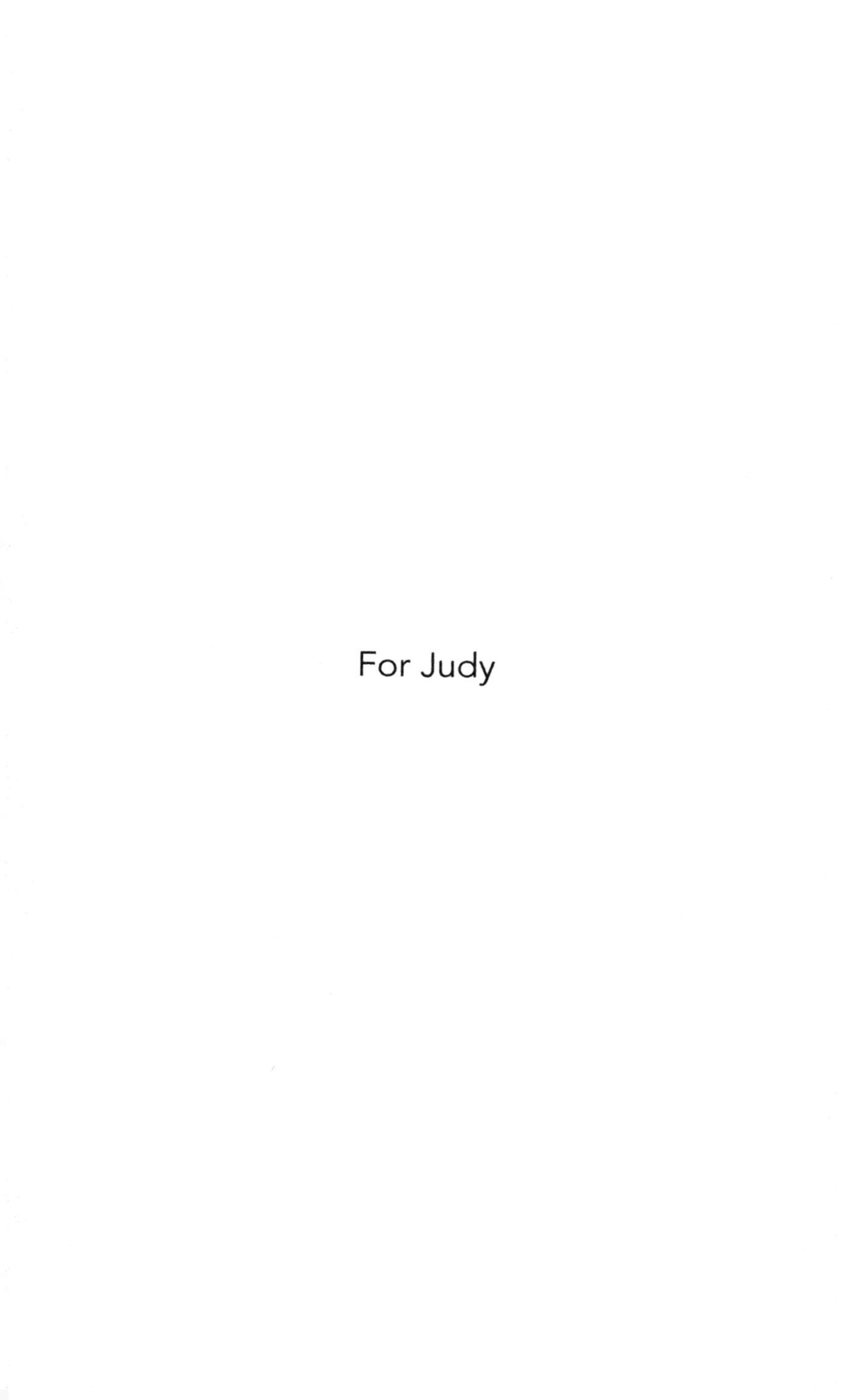

For Judy

Welcome!

Hi friend!

I am so glad you are going to join me on this adventure called life. Life can get pretty crazy, am I right? There are many voices demanding your attention. Voices that tell you how to look, how to dress, who to be, what to believe in. And just as you figure out the look you want or the group you want to be a part of, the rules change, and you're left once again to figure out where you fit in.

How do you know which is the right voice or the right idea? How do you know which voice to listen to? As you read through these pages, it's my hope that you will know which voice you can always trust: God's. It's my prayer that you will grow in your understanding of what it means to be a child of God, a daughter of the King. Sound good to you? Keep reading.

Maybe you're wondering why I've named this series "Bloom." Well, in nature, there is beauty in each stage of a flower blooming. From a tight bud, to unfurled petals in all their glory, there is beauty. I want you to know there is beauty in each stage of growing up. Yes, you will experience awkward and uncomfortable times during these years, but be encouraged! You are lovely in God's sight, no matter what's happened during the day. There is nothing you can do (or not do) to make you unlovely in God's sight. He loves to look down on his garden to smile at his children growing at different times and in different ways.

Here's how this book works. Each day there will be a scripture to read and a few thoughts to help you apply that scripture to your life.

In the "What About Me" section, sometimes there will be a question, prayer, or action for you to take. Sometimes, there won't be anything but a blank space, and you can use that to write whatever is on your heart and share it with God. It's your space.

My prayer is that this book becomes like a friend, accompanying you on your journey to blooming into the young woman God desires. May it encourage you to open into the lovely flower the Lord created you to be.

Are you ready to bloom?

Part 1:

Who is God?

Getting Started

This first part is called "Who is God?" In this section, you'll learn who God is and what he wants to do in your life. It's hard to have a relationship with someone if you don't even know them, right? Just like you know your friend's favorite band, favorite Starbucks drink, and favorite go-to outfit, Jesus wants us to get to know him, details and all. So this section will be all about getting to know who Jesus really is. Grab your favorite Starbucks drink and settle in. It's going to be a great ride.

Day 1: My Savior

In Genesis 3, at the beginning of the Bible, we find the story of Adam and Eve. Adam and Eve are having a bad day. They were the first humans created, and God had provided for everything they could ever need. They were perfect and had close fellowship with God himself. They had each other, a beautiful garden and zoo to take care of, and lots of love and peace.

They had all of this and only a few rules, but they chose to disobey the rules. They decided they were smarter than God. Bad choice.

Because they made that decision, they were no longer perfect.

But God created humans and still wanted to have a relationship with them. So what now?

Instead of leaving Adam and Eve, and ultimately us to fend for ourselves, he made a way to save us by sending his son, Jesus, to the Earth. Even though Adam and Eve (and therefore every human after them) messed up, even though it was our own fault, even though sin left a horrible stain on us, God didn't cut us off.

"For God so loved the world, that he gave

his only Son, that whoever believes in him

should not perish, but have eternal life. For
God did not send his Son into the world to
condemn the world, but in order that the
world might be saved through him."

John 3:16-17

He loved us so much that he sent his son, his very own son to take our punishment. He made a way for us to still have a relationship with him.

What about me?

I learned that God loves me very much and wants to be my savior!

Day 2: Finders Keepers

I love gifts. I love giving gifts and getting gifts. It's one of the ways I show people that I care about them and love them. I want you to think about your favorite gift you've ever received. Got it? Now think about how you would feel if you lost this gift. How terrible, right? You would look and look until you found it. Then you would probably be happy when you found it.

Did you know the Bible says we are all lost and in need of being found? Let's look in Luke 19 to find out more.

"For the Son of Man came to seek and to

save the lost."

Luke 19:10

God knew we couldn't find our way back to him on our own, so that's why he sent his son Jesus to find us. We were so lost, we'd never be able to find our way back to God, even with Google Maps! He is such a good God. He didn't have to sacrifice his own son to find us and save us, but he did.

And when he finds us, he shouts "Finders Keepers!" And never lets us go.

What about me?

Take an index card and write in big letters, "I AM FOUND," and place it somewhere where you will see it every day. Let that be a reminder that God will never lose track of you.

Day 3: So Bright!

Did you know the angels in heaven have different jobs to do? Some angels bring messages to God's people, others do battle in the heavens and still others praise and worship God night and day.

One of the songs sung before God's throne by the angels is "Holy, holy, holy." What does holy even mean? When something is holy, that means it is pure, clean and perfect. To be holy is to be set apart.

"Holy, holy, holy is the Lord God Almighty,

who was, and is, and is to come."

Revelation 4:8b

Whenever the Bible says something, we know it's important. Whenever the Bible repeats something, we know it's really important. And whenever the Bible says something three times, you better highlight it, put a sticky note there, and remember it, because it's super important.

God is most holy and cannot be around anything less than pure. Anything less than holy would melt away like an ice cube under bright sunshine on a hot sidewalk. God's holiness is like the bright sunshine. We can't look directly at it, even while we're wearing sunglasses.

What about me?

Next time you hear a worship song, listen for words and phrases declaring that God is holy. The next time you slip on a pair of sunglasses, thank God for his holiness.

Day 4: Daddy

What do you call your father? Dad? Daddy? Papa? Something else? I am married and have my own house, but I will always be his little girl. Out of affection, I like calling him "Daddy."

Throughout the Bible, God is called our heavenly father and we are called his children.

Even though God is big and powerful, he calls us his children. This truth should make me and you feel safe, protected, and valued.

Maybe, though, your earthly parents don't make you feel like you're treasured, and it's hard imagining God making you feel safe and valued. Earthly parents make mistakes, but God does not. He loves you perfectly, all the time for the rest of time. You can trust this promise.

"See what great love the Father has lavished

on us, that we should be called children of

God! And that is what we are!"

1 John 3:1

What about me?

To better understand this concept of God, start your prayers this week by praying *"Dear heavenly Daddy" or "heavenly father"*—something to remind you God is your father. Might that change how you pray? Might that make you feel more relaxed and safe? Journal your thoughts here at the end of the week.

Day 5: Good Gifts

"Which of you fathers, if your son asks for a fish, will give him a snake instead? Or if he asks for an egg, will give him a scorpion? If you then, though you are evil, know how to give good gifts to your children, how much more will your Father in heaven give the Holy Spirit to those who ask him!"

Luke 11:11-13

Eggs and scorpions? What is this scripture talking about? Chances are, if you ask your dad for an ice cream cone, he isn't going to give you a raw onion. Gross! Or, if you ask for new shoes, your mom isn't going to give you a mouse. That would be crazy!

This scripture states that if even our earthly parents know how to give their children good and helpful gifts, how much more does God know how to provide for his children?

No matter what you go through in life, no matter whether you're going through tough times or great times, God knows how to provide for you. And you can be assured he gives good gifts to his kids.

What about me?

In the space below, list some "good things" that God has filled your life with.

Day 6: Because He Loves Us

Raise your hand if you've ever gotten in trouble with your parents.

It happens to all of us. They ask us to do (or not do) something, and we fail to listen and obey. Most of the time, consequences follow such a choice. Loss of privileges, grounding, or maybe even a spanking can result from disobedience.

But here's a little secret. When we're disciplined for doing something wrong, our parents do it for our own good. I know it may not seem like that at the time, but it's true! They don't get pleasure out of it -- in fact, most of the time, it hurts them more than it hurts us. But they discipline, anyway, because they want you to grow up and be a strong, healthy adult.

If they don't discipline you, they aren't doing you any favors. In fact, it's more hurtful to you if they don't discipline you. Crazy, I know. The Bible says God operates in the same way.

"Moreover, we have all had human fathers who disciplined us and we respected them for it. How much more should we submit to the Father of spirits and live! They disciplined us for a little while as they

thought best; but God disciplines us for our

good, in order that we may share in his

holiness. No discipline seems pleasant at

the time, but painful. Later on, however, it

produces a harvest of righteousness and

peace for those who have been trained by

it."

Hebrews 12:9-11

We can trust that when God (or our parents) disciplines us, it's because they love us. They love us a lot. Let's practice having a teachable heart, and let's try to obey the first time.

What about me?

Is there something your parents have asked you to do that you haven't done yet? Or maybe something that God is asking you to do? Pray and ask that he would give you the strength to do those very things, and then do them!

Day 7: Friend of God

Think of someone famous you would love to become friends with. A musician, a sports star, or a movie star – it could be anyone. Are you thinking?

Do you realize you can be friends with the coolest person ever, right now?

"I no longer call you servants, because a servant does not know his master's business. Instead, I have called you friends, for everything that I learned from my Father I have made known to you."

John 15:15

We can be friends with God. The God of the universe! The one we've been learning about who is also our Savior and our Father.

The scripture above is from Jesus' last few hours before his crucifixion. He was talking with his disciples, a small group of men who learned and worked with Jesus. Jesus told them they were not just servants, but also friends. Because they heard these messages from God, he reminded them that all who were his friends followed his commandments. The title of *friend* is backed up by action.

But this promise wasn't just for Jesus' disciples. This is an incredible promise that applies to all of us, and it's one that should encourage us. The God of the whole world wants to be our friend. Even though he has massive amounts of angels to be friends with, he chooses us humans to be friends with, too. When we obey God, when we love others with our words and actions, we demonstrate that we are God's friends.

What about me?

The next time you hang out with your friends, remember that God wants to spend time with you as a friend too!

Day 8: Clouds

In the Old Testament, God directed the Israelites for part of their journey to the Promised Land with a pillar of cloud and a pillar of fire. When the pillar moved, they moved campsites. When the pillar stayed, they stayed too.

The cloud was a fixture of their daily lives. Many mornings would have consisted of them pulling back the edge of their tent and gazing toward the tabernacle to learn what the day would hold: assigning the kids to help take down the tent or tending the flocks as usual. Whichever it was, they followed.

Do you know that God speaks to you and guides you? Do you tune into him each day to find out what he wants you to do? While we may not have a massive cloud of smoke and fire telling us what to do, God always knows how to talk to his children in a way they understand. It takes practice to listen and to tune into what God is saying.

"So the cloud of the Lord was over the

tabernacle by day, and fire was in the cloud

by night, in the sight of all the Israelites

during all their travels."

Exodus 40:38

What about me?

Cut out a picture of a cloud or campfire from a magazine and place it in your Bible to remind you that God speaks to you, and he wants you to follow him, no matter what.

Day 9: My Healer

God is the creator of the universe and the designer of our bodies. He knows how our brains and hearts work. He knows how the bones in our toes fit together, and how the red blood cells move throughout our veins. He created the DNA that would determine if we had blue eyes or green ones, if we would be short or tall, if we would have straight hair or curly hair.

But you may wonder if he has all of this knowledge, why do bad things still happen, like people getting sick?

The reason is we live in a fallen world with sin, a world where illness and injuries happen, but not because God causes it or is punishing his kids. He already did all of the punishing while Jesus was on the cross.

If you or someone close to you is sick or hurt, you can always carry those burdens to God in prayer. God is a God who heals, whether it's healing here on earth, or complete healing in heaven.

Sickness and death are part of this world here, but we can also look forward to life in heaven where there is no sickness or death. In both places (on earth and heaven) God takes perfect care of his kids. We can trust that God loves us perfectly, and nothing is too difficult for him.

"Was my arm too short to deliver you? Do I

lack the strength to rescue you?"

Isaiah 50:2b

God's arm is not too short to reach us where we are and it is not lacking in strength to heal us. What a strong promise to rest in.

What about me?

Are you sick, or does someone that you know need prayer for healing? Write your name or their names below and spend some time talking to God about it.

Day 10: My Shepherd

"The Lord is my shepherd, I lack nothing."

Psalm 23:1

This is the opening verse to one of the more well-known psalms, Psalm 23.

King David, a shepherd boy-turned-king, is responsible for these six beautiful verses. He knew enough about sheep to know what he was saying as he compared God to a shepherd and us to sheep.

Sheep can't provide for themselves and need (and want) direction every day, even as they travel over familiar paths. They trust their shepherd's guiding hand.

Maybe there is a lot you need and want in life. Maybe for whatever reason your family and loved ones can't provide everything you need. This verse encourages me in many seasons because it reminds me that, since God is my shepherd, God is the one who is taking care of me, so I do not lack anything. He supplies my every need.

He lets us rest in good places and keeps us safe in bad places. He pours blessing over us, even when those blessings are unexpected. When you acknowledge God is your shepherd, you are acknowledging some of the basic truths about following God and finding your identity in him.

What about me?

Write out Psalm 23:1 on a notecard and put it where you'll see it regularly. Let it be a reminder that God is taking care of all of your needs.

Day 11: One Voice

Another key in the relationship between a shepherd and his sheep is how the sheep listen to his voice. They are trained to follow him and him alone. They move when they hear his voice, and stay put when his voice is silent.

Impostors may try to deceive the sheep, but they know their real shepherd. And they don't sway from his voice. As children of God, we are called to develop the same intense listening and following skills, tuning into God's voice and not the world's. God's directions are for our benefit, always growing us into Christ's image.

The voice of the world does not always have our best interests at heart. The voice of the world can deceive, discourage, and destroy. God's voice tells the truth, encourages, and builds.

"When he has brought out all his own, he goes on ahead of them, and his sheep follow him because they know his voice. But they will never follow a stranger; in fact, they will run away from him because they do not

recognize a stranger's voice."

John 10:4-5

What about me?

Do you know the voice of the Shepherd? Do you follow his commands?

Let's practice our sheep listening skills and follow only the Great Shepherd, Jesus.

Day 12: At What Cost?

The true shepherd goes to great lengths to protect and care for his flock. An impostor or even a hired hand isn't invested like the shepherd who daily cares, feeds, and guides each and every sheep. Impostors could care less what happens to this squirmy flock of sheep.

The true shepherd sets out in search of stray lambs and even puts his own body in harm's way to take care of his flock.

The Bible says Jesus, our great shepherd, has done the same thing for us. He laid down his life for us so we might be safe and have eternal life.

No one else has done that or will do that. Only Jesus can claim that kind of sacrifice.

We are so loved as children of God that our Shepherd would put himself in harm's way just so we are kept safe. To me, there is no greater proof Jesus is who he says he is than this truth.

"I am the good shepherd; I know my

sheep and my sheep know me— just as the

Father knows me and I know the Father—

and I lay down my life for the sheep...My

sheep listen to my voice; I know them, and

they follow me. I give them eternal life, and

they shall never perish; no one will snatch

them out of my hand."

John 10:14-15, 27-28

What about me?

In the space below, write out a short prayer thanking the Lord for how he leads you and protects you.

Day 13: Carried in His Arms

For the first several months of our lives, our mothers carry us in their bodies. Day and night, their bodies help to nourish and grow ours. More than we know, this process causes them discomfort and pain, but they wouldn't trade a single moment because they know soon they will get to hold their beautiful babies.

Then for the first few years of our lives, we spend a lot of time in our parents' and other caregivers' arms. We can't walk on our own. We tire and frighten easily, and we need help to do everyday tasks.

Our parents have their own burdens to carry, but because of how much they love us, they take us into their arms and lovingly give us what we need.

"He tends his flock like a shepherd: He gathers the lambs in his arms and carries them close to his heart; he gently leads those that have young."

Isaiah 40:11

The scripture reminds us that God our shepherd carries us close to his heart. I can't think of a safer place to be. And the best part is, God's arms will never tire of carrying us. He is forever strong.

What about me?

If you have a baby brother or sister, think about how much time your parents spend carrying them around. Thank your God for carrying you every day!

Day 14: Angry No More

Do you every wonder if God is angry with you or holds a grudge against you? It's a common question, but an important one.

Jesus appears on the scene in the New Testament, perfect and sinless. He pays the price for our sins, and God's wrath is poured out on Him. Not us. But Jesus.

God is not angry at us. He is not waiting for us to make a mistake. He has already dealt out the punishment for our sins.

As children of God, we shouldn't be afraid of him like we are waiting to be grounded or even spanked. The punishment has already been given.

God does not punish his children with tragedy, sickness, or accidents. We still live in a fallen world with other sinful people. But it's not God's fault. He did not cause it. His anger was poured out as Jesus lay dying on the cross, and then it was satisfied. He is angry with us no more.

"Since we have now been justified by his blood, how much more shall we be saved from God's wrath through him! For if, while we were God's enemies, we were reconciled

to him through the death of his Son, how

much more, having been reconciled, shall we

be saved through his life!?"

Romans 5:9-10

What about me?

Stand in front of a mirror and make the angriest face you can. Now turn that frown into your biggest smile and thank God that he is angry with us no more!

Day 15: He Loves You

My prayer for you today is that you would begin to understand how much you are loved by God. He gave his only son for you. If you were the only person in the world, he still would've sent his son, Jesus. You are loved. You have purpose. You are precious.

Knowing how much you are loved should change how you look at the world. No longer should you feel fearful and insignificant. You are the daughter of THE king. You are bold and powerful. You are on a mission and God equips you for whatever you will face.

"And I pray that you, being rooted and

established in love, may have power,

together with all the Lord's holy people, to

grasp how wide and long and high and

deep is the love of Christ, and to know this

love that surpasses knowledge—that you

may be filled to the measure of all the

fullness of God."

Ephesians 3:17b-19

You are filled with Jesus, dear sisters in Christ. Now go change the world.

What about me?

Day 16: Rainbows

You can learn a lot about a person by the promises they make (or break, for that matter). God makes many promises to his kids in the Bible, and guess what? He keeps them all. Always—for all time.

One of his beautiful promises is that of a rainbow. A few generations after creation, humans were still making sinful, horrible decisions, and God destroyed all but one family from the earth. Noah's was the only righteous family.

After the flood, God put his rainbow in the sky as a promise to not destroy the earth with a flood again.

Where I live, we often have severe weather during springtime. Tornadoes fire up on humid afternoons when the conditions are just right. They are quick, fierce, and destructive.

Last night was one of those storms. The tornadoes weren't as fierce as they could have been, but buildings were heavily damaged and cars turned over. Storms are never fun.

But after the rain and hail had stopped, after the tornadoes dissipated back into the sky, there was not one, but two rainbows arching up above. What a beautiful sight.

Whenever I see them, I am reminded of God's faithfulness, even during storms. I am thankful to serve a God like that.

"Whenever the rainbow appears in the clouds, I will see it and remember the everlasting covenant between God and all living creatures of every kind on the earth."

Genesis 9:16

What about me?

In the space below, draw a rainbow. Let it be a reminder that God is always faithful to keep his promises.

Day 17: Knowing God

There is a difference between knowing someone and knowing *about* someone, right?

For instance, if we were to meet someday, and I were to tell you about my best friend Leah, you would know *about* Leah, but you wouldn't know her personally.

I could also tell you about my lovely sisters-in-law, Hilary and Morgan, but you would only know about them, you wouldn't know them personally

Unfortunately, some people think it's different when it comes to God. They think knowing *about* God is the same as *knowing* him, the same as having a relationship with Him.

That's just not true. Hearing other people talk about Jesus, going to church and knowing a few worship songs, doesn't count as knowing Jesus personally. And knowing Jesus personally is what guarantees eternal life.

"Not everyone who says to me, 'Lord, Lord,' will enter the kingdom of heaven, but only the one who does the will of my Father who is in heaven. Many will say to me on that day, 'Lord, Lord, did we not prophesy in your name and in your name drive out demons

and in your name perform many miracles?'

Then I will tell them plainly, 'I never knew

you. Away from me, you evildoers!"

Matthew 7:21-23

What about me?

As you have spent time learning about who God is over the past couple of weeks, maybe it's helped to strengthen the relationship you already have with him. The very thought makes me so happy.

Or maybe you realize you don't have a relationship with him but want to make that decision. If that's a decision you want to make, feel free to pray the prayer below in your own words. Then, tell a caring Christian adult about your decision. They'll help you with the next steps.

Pray this with me:

Dear Jesus, I don't want to just know about you, but I want to know you personally. I know you came and died for my sins and rose again so I could have a personal relationship with you. Thank you. Come into my heart now and make me your kid. Help me to follow you every day. I love you. Thank you for loving me.

In Jesus' name, amen.

[illegible] out his arms [illegible]

and in your [illegible]

[illegible] will [illegible]

You. Away [illegible]

Matthew 25:23

[illegible]

As you have spent time learning about what [illegible] the best [illegible] as you [illegible] relationship [illegible] you [illegible] Then every [illegible] happy, [illegible] relationship with him [illegible] that's a conclusion you want to make [illegible] today [illegible] below in your own words [illegible] Questions [illegible] they'll help you [illegible]

[illegible]

Dear Jesus, I don't want to [illegible] want to know [illegible] and died for my sins and rose again [illegible] with you [illegible] my heart now [illegible] to follow [illegible]

[illegible] name, Amen.

[illegible]

Part 2:

How Do You View Yourself?

Getting Started

This second part is called "How Do You View Yourself?" In this section, you'll be learning about how to have a healthy self-image and finding out who you are in Christ. It's tough being a girl sometimes, isn't it? So many people are telling us who to be, what to wear, how to do our hair. Sometimes you just need to take a step back and listen to what God says. He already thinks you are beautiful and precious, no Instagram or Snapchat filter needed. This section will encourage you to be the young woman that God has called you to be and will help you grow in your confidence. Let's jump in!

Day 18: Made in the Image of God

How would you describe yourself? Do you look more like your mom or your dad? Do you have a twin?

I have brown eyes and long, light brown hair. I look a little bit like my dad and a little bit like my mom. My brother is much taller than I am, and he looks a lot like my dad.

It's neat to see the variety God uses when he creates people. Some people are taller, some are shorter. Some have curly red hair. Others have long blond hair. Some have green eyes, some have blue eyes. His creativity is endless!

Not one person looks the same as another, and that's OK. Variety is beautiful. God is so creative when he makes us humans.

"So God created mankind in his own

image, in the image of God he created

them; male and female he created them."

Genesis 1:27

In the beginning of the Bible, we learn that not only did God create men and women, he created them in his own image, meaning he used himself as a pattern for humans. And that should encourage us!

Sometimes when other kids look different than us or we think we look different than everyone else, the differences make us scared or sad. Or maybe we just wished we looked different, that we did have longer hair, or shorter hair. Or that we were taller, or had a different-shaped nose. The good news is we don't have to feel or think that way.

Remember we are all made in the image of God, and that makes us each very special. God doesn't make mistakes.

What about me?

With your parents' permission, tape or glue a picture of yourself in the space below. Thank God that he made you just how he wanted to!

Day 19: You're On My Team!

Imagine God visited your school one day and came to teach your P.E. class. That would be a crazy day—a crazy cool day. Pretend God is picking teams for a basketball game. Who do you think is going to be on his team?

Do you think the boy who is tallest and best at free throws will get picked first? What about the girl who runs the fastest in all of sixth grade?

Can I tell you a secret? God would choose all of you. He wants everyone on his team.

"I took you from the ends of the earth, from its farthest corners I called you. I said, 'You are my servant'; I have chosen you and have not rejected you."

Isaiah 41:9

In life, it may seem like we get passed over for different reasons. Another girl gets the part in the musical you wanted, someone else gets picked first for dodge ball, your sibling gets to go on a cool trip and you don't. The teacher calls on that other girl *again* to answer a question in class.

If you are a child of God, you are hand–picked by God to fulfill his plan. He didn't pass you over and pick someone else, he wants you—yes, you.

The fact that the God of the universe has chosen you to do awesome works for his kingdom should fill you with courage.

What about me?

Pray this with me:

God, thank you that I get to be on your team. That makes me feel special. Help me to listen to you so I can know you better and know what you want me to do. Help me to grow as a member of your team. I love you, Lord, and I know you love me too.

In Jesus' name, amen.

Day 20: A Beautiful Heart

Your heart can perform some amazing feats.

- The heart pumps 100 gallons of blood through the body each hour, enough to fill 1,600 drinking glasses.
- A person's heart may beat 3.5 billion times in a lifetime.
- Men and women's hearts beat differently. A women's heartbeat is faster (78 beats per minute) than a man's (70 beats per minute).

All of this is hidden inside your body; you can't see it working, but it's still important. We couldn't live without our hearts doing their jobs.

The same thing is true for our spiritual hearts as we learn to love and follow after Jesus. We can't see it, but it's so important that it does its job.

The world we live in can put a lot of focus on our outsides. What does our hairstyle say about us, are our clothes the most fashionable, do we look a certain way?

Even among people we know, sometimes it's hard not to focus on how someone looks and yearn to be more like them, or wish we didn't look the way we look.

"Charm is deceptive, and beauty is fleeting;

but a woman who fears the Lord is to be

praised."

Proverbs 31:30

God's word says our outer looks change and pass away, but the beauty we've cultivated on the inside is truly worthy of modeling. And while there is nothing wrong with enjoying a new outfit or a new hairstyle or a new nail polish, remember to make your heart pretty by loving God and others, using kind words, and thinking of others first.

What about me?

In the space below, draw a heart. It can be big or small, fancy or simple. Remember that it's so much more important that our heart is pretty than it is that our outsides are attractive.

Day 21: A Work in Progress

Imagine drawing or painting a picture, and that while you're drawing it, your friend looks over your shoulder. The drawing clearly isn't finished, but your friend starts criticizing your work.

"Why is that blank space there? That's doesn't look pretty."

"I don't like these colors."

"Those shapes are weird. I don't think it will look good."

The picture isn't even done. How can anyone comment on how it looks if they aren't seeing the finished product?

Too often, though, we do the same thing with others—and with ourselves. We feel like we can judge and make comments on people's lives when they are still works in progress. Or maybe we are too harsh with ourselves, not realizing God is working on us, too.

"...being confident of this, that he who began a good work in you will carry it on to completion until the day of Christ Jesus."

Philippians 1:6

God will not leave you unfinished and incomplete. This scripture is always so encouraging when I'm having a bad day because I realize God is not upset with me; he is molding me into a daughter of the king. And he's not finished yet.

What about me?

The next time you're tempted to judge an unfinished masterpiece in yourself or others, remember these scriptures. God will fulfill and complete that which he has started in us. That's a promise.

Day 22: Modesty Starts Within

If we are daughters of the king, that makes us, well...royal. Have you ever thought about that? How does being "royal" affect our day-to-day lives? One thing it affects is modesty. How should a royal daughter dress?

I'm know each family has its own set of rules about what is appropriate and what is not appropriate to wear. I know I did growing up, and I still abide by some of the same guidelines.

Maybe your shorts have to be a certain length; maybe you don't get to wear shorts at all. Maybe you can't wear high heels yet. Maybe you can only wear a one-piece bathing suit or a tankini, but not a bikini. Maybe you can wear spaghetti-strap tops to the lake, but not to church.

Whatever clothing guidelines your parents or guardians have set, remember modesty is not just about the clothes. Modesty is also an attitude of the heart, and our heavenly Father can always see that attitude.

Our culture tries to tell us less is more: less clothing, less modesty, less thoughtfulness is more cool or more appealing. That's simply not true though. Let's go to God's Word and see what he says.

"What matters is not your outer appearance—the styling of your hair, the jewelry you wear, the cut of your clothes—but your inner disposition. Cultivate inner beauty, the gentle, gracious kind that God delights in."

1 Peter 3:3-4 (MSG)

Every body shape is different, every family is different, but God calls *all* of his daughters to cultivate inner beauty—that's what matters.

What about me?

Whether you are happy or unhappy with what you wear (or aren't allowed to wear) remember, you are no ordinary girl. A daughter of the king has a different call on her life. Your example of modesty and inner beauty will shine bright in a dark world—not to make anybody else look bad, but to show them a new way of living.

Day 23: The Temple

"Do you not know that your bodies are temples of the Holy Spirit, who is in you, whom you have received from God? You are not your own; you were bought at a price. Therefore honor God with your bodies."

1 Corinthians 6:19-20

This special verse gives us a standard of how we are to treat our earthly dwellings, our bodies.

It says our bodies are actual temples or living spaces of the Holy Spirit. This is representative of the temple in the Old Testament, the place where God's people were able to connect with Him. God's presence dwelled in the inner most part of the temple, and let me tell you, it was a very special place.

The priests and the rest of the Jews who came into the temple treated it with the upmost respect.

They didn't draw graffiti on the walls, skateboard in the courtyard, or drip ice cream on the rug. They knew it was the living space of God and treated it accordingly.

The same is now true for our bodies. Once Jesus ascended back into heaven, he sent the Holy Spirit to live with—and within—each believer.

Our culture sends a lot of messages about what we can do with our bodies: feed it bad food, not feed it enough, hurt it, or just talk down on it.

When we remind ourselves, as children of God, that the Holy Spirit lives in us, how does that change how we view our bodies? Treat our bodies? Talk about our bodies to other believers? God wants us to honor him with our bodies because he did pay a high price so we might have life. Treat your body with kindness and speak good words about it.

What about me?

Pray this with me:

Lord, thank you for my body. I thank you that you want me to be healthy and strong. Help me to take good care of my body and always speak kind words about it. Help me to encourage my friends to treat their bodies well too.

In Jesus' name, amen.

Day 24: Flowers in the Field

My mother-in-law is a fabulous gardener. I wish you could see her flower beds. Flowers, bushes, trees, and grasses of all sorts adorn her front and back yards.

From time to time, she helps me pick out flowers for my yard, and I'm always amazed at the variety of flowers and plants covering this beautiful planet. Shapes, colors, smells—there is not one the same as the next. God has even given his children the creativity to blend plants together to make brand new ones.

If there is that much creativity in creation, think about how much God enjoys diversity in his children. We are all so different, and it makes life beautiful. Life would be boring if we all looked, dressed, and talked the same.

Instead of being afraid of differences, we should embrace them. Our differences reflect God's diversity. He loves his creation and wants us to enjoy it.

"See how the flowers of the field grow. They

do not labor or spin. Yet I tell you that not

even Solomon in all his splendor was

dressed like one of these."

Matthew 6:28b-29

What about me?

In the space below, draw a bouquet of flowers. Or, with an adult's help, buy a bouquet of fresh flowers or pick some from a garden and place it somewhere in your home. Thank God for all the variety in nature!

Day 25: God's Favorite

We all love the feeling of being someone's "favorite." We love being a BFF, being closest to Grandma, or having more artwork on the fridge at home. It's human nature to enjoy the spotlight, in some form or another.

Guess what? You are God's favorite.

"Since you are precious and honored in my sight, and because I love you, I will give people in exchange for you, nations in exchange for your life."

Isaiah 43:4

Because God is God and is not like us, he has the capacity to call each child his "favorite." We are precious and honored in his sight.

It doesn't matter if you sit at the cool table at lunch, get a lot of likes on Instagram, or have a ton of Snapchat followers, you are already popular with the coolest person ever. Jesus.

If that doesn't put a smile on your face...well, I'm not sure what will. Live confidently knowing you are precious in God's sight.

What about me?

In the space below, write out in big letters "I AM GOD'S FAVORITE."

Never forget that you are precious in God's eyes and that he loves you very much. Nothing can snatch you out of his hands or change his mind.

Day 26: 1 of 1

If you look closely at an original drawing or painting, sometimes you can see two numbers divided by a slash:

84/500

30/100

1/1

Do you know what these numbers mean? These numbers let you know how many of this drawing or painting there are and which one you're looking at; for example, there were 500 of one particular painting, and you're looking at the 84th one.

When people look at you, they are looking at 1 of 1, the only one made of its kind. God didn't use any other people to copy when he made you. He made you distinctly unique. There are no other copies like you in the whole history of the world.

Why do we try to be the same as one another? Maybe, just maybe, it hurts God's feelings when his beautiful children look in the mirror and decide, "I'm not good enough. I need to be more like so-and-so."

Don't make that choice. You are enough, just the way you are. Be you and only you.

"I praise you because I am fearfully and

wonderfully made..."

Psalm 139: 14a

What about me?

When we acknowledge that we are wonderfully made, it's a way to praise God. The opposite is also true. When we are unkind to ourselves, it doesn't honor God. Your family, your church, your school—the whole world—needs you as God created you, not more faked and forced copies of someone else.

You are a unique masterpiece of God; how does that make you feel?

Day 27: Crowned with Glory and Honor

We all have people in our lives who are a little bit different from us. Maybe you think you are the one who is different from all your friends. This variety is what makes life beautiful and exciting.

But just because someone is a little different doesn't mean you should be afraid of them. God's Word says we are made in the image of God, and we have worth based on this fact alone.

"what is mankind that you are mindful of them, human beings that you care for them? You have made them a little lower than the angels and crowned them with glory and honor. You made them rulers over the works of your hands; you put everything under their feet."

Psalm 8:4-6

This scripture even says we are crowned with glory and honor. That sounds royal!

Maybe you have autism, have to use a wheelchair, or have a learning disability. If not you, then maybe you know somebody who deals with something like that. Being around someone who is not like us can sometimes make us nervous.

We shouldn't react in fear and meanness, though. That person is crowned with the glory and honor of God, same as you.

What about me?

Does that change how you feel about yourself? How you look at others? As you interact with the people in your life, remember that God has crowned them with glory and honor. Everyone is worthy of kind words and actions.

Day 28: Just Right

Does it ever feel like you are too young to do all the activities you want to do, all that things that seem super fun?

You don't get to stay up as late as your older sister, you aren't old enough to drive yet, maybe you can't get your ears pierced yet.

Too young, not old enough. Not yet.

I tired of hearing those words when I was a kid. I wanted to be able to do cool things *now*.

In the Bible, God often uses young people to do great work in his kingdom. In the opening pages of Jeremiah, we find God giving a young man an important job. Jeremiah was a prophet. A prophet listens to God and shares special messages with God's people.

Jeremiah was young; he says so himself in Jeremiah 1:6, "I am only a youth…" But God reminds him to focus not on his circumstances, but on the one who made him.

"But the Lord said to me, "Do not say, 'I am too young.' You must go to everyone I send you to and say whatever I command you. Do not be afraid of them, for I am with you and will rescue you," declares the Lord. Then the Lord reached out his hand and touched my mouth and said to me, "I have put my words in your mouth."

Jeremiah 1:7-9

God didn't want any of Jeremiah's excuses. For Jeremiah to make excuses made it sound like God had made a mistake. God never makes mistakes. So just like Jeremiah, we can be encouraged when God calls us to do something. He never has the wrong number. He hasn't picked the "wrong person." He wants you.

What about me?

In the space below, write out some things that you are good at or enjoy doing. Pray and ask God to show you how he can use your talents and skills, even now, to do great things for him.

Day 29: The Truth

Did you know Satan our enemy can't tell the truth? It's against his nature to be truthful.

"He was a murderer from the beginning, not holding to the truth, for there is no truth in him. When he lies, he speaks his native language, for he is a liar and the father of lies."

John 8:44b

That's powerful. Often, the enemy whispers lies in our ears, which sound like they could be true.

"You know they're talking about you…they say they're your friends, but they don't like you."

"You're not pretty enough."

"You're too fat."

"Ugh, your nose is weird."

"You're a loser."

Based on the scripture above, we can recognize these statements as lies, and we can reject them. Part of growing in God's garden is learning to recognize truth and soaking it up like water and sunshine. At the same time, we must learn to recognize lies and fend them off like dirty bugs that feast on our beautiful leaves.

Bugs and disease ruin plants; water and sunshine make them grow strong. God's truth will always nourish us and keep us strong. The enemy's lies only weaken us.

The only way to better recognize lies is to consistently dig into God's word. The more you read and study the truth, the easier it is to recognize a lie. Whenever I get discouraged and fearful, I step back and look at my thoughts. I remind myself Satan is incapable of telling the whole truth, so I reject those thoughts that are from him, and I turn to God's thoughts. Then I feel strong and brave again.

God's desire is for us is to be victorious. Listen to the soundtrack of his truth.

What about me?

Pray this with me:

God, help me as I learn to recognize your truth, and reject the enemy's lies. I know that Satan can't tell me anything good. Help me to close my ears to him, and open my ears to you.

In Jesus' name, amen.

Day 30: Compliments Are Free

As girls, it can be easy to get jealous of one another and put each other down to make ourselves feel better. Even if it's just small digs, they can do great damage to tender, growing hearts.

A story I read with my grandmother has stuck with me. When a person lights one candle with another, the flame of the first candle doesn't diminish. In the same way, complimenting someone else or someone else's victories don't make you less. Giving compliments cost you nothing. They won't make you "poorer." They will make you richer.

"A generous person will prosper; whoever

refreshes others will be refreshed."

Proverbs 11:25

Perhaps you can't be generous with money yet, but I bet you can be generous with smiles and encouragement. There are many ways to be generous that have nothing to do with money. And you may find that it makes you just as happy as the person you are helping.

What about me?

I promise you there are girls who cross paths with you every week who could use an extra smile or a kind word. Will you give this encouragement to them? Remember, it costs you nothing. But it may mean everything to someone else.

Day 31: Not Too Busy

"Sweetie, hang on a minute, I'm on the phone."

"Gah, get out of my room! I don't have time for your baby stuff!"

"Not right now. Now is not a good time."

Every hear phrases like these from your parents or older siblings? We want to know people have time for us, and it hurts our feelings just a little bit (or a lot) when they don't appear to have time to listen to us or help us.

I have good news for you. God is never too busy to listen to or help you.

"Cast all your anxiety on him because he

cares for you."

1 Peter 5:7

This verse gives us the picture of taking whatever is too big for our hands and giving it to God. He is not too busy, and he doesn't think our troubles are too little or insignificant. He is bending down, ready to take our burdens and to listen.

Whether you've had a fight with your friend, you're in trouble with a teacher, or your heart is just a little sad, God cares. And He is listening. He is not too busy for you.

Day 32: Number the Stars

Have you ever looked up at the sky on a clear night, far away from the city? Sometimes the lights make it hard to see all the twinkly stars. But when you get away from all that light pollution, you'll realize there were millions more stars you didn't even know existed.

On the volcano Mauna Kea in Hawaii, they have a large viewing area at the visitors' center. The first time I was there, it was early January, and there were so many stars dotting the night sky, it was unbelievable. I thought I had seen a lot of stars before, but I was wrong. The sky with all the shimmering, twinkling lights was breathtaking.

Why all this talk about stars? There's beautiful scripture near the end of Psalm which makes this declaration about God:

"He determines the number of the stars and

calls them each by name."

Psalm 147:4

God can count the stars…and he's named them.

If God pays that kind of attention to stars, how much more do you think he is paying attention to the details of your life? If he has named all the stars, you can be sure he will not forget about you.

He sees you. He loves you. And He will never leave you.

What about me?

Before you go to bed one night, step out on your front porch (with an adults' permission) and look up at the stars. Just try to count them. It's impossible! Thank God that he who is able to keep track of details like stars is also fully capable of keeping track of your life!

Day 33: A New Creation

Ashlyn knelt down in front of the flower pot on her family's back porch, a tiny stick captivating her attention. A butterfly chrysalis, or cocoon, adorned the side of a slender stick. The butterfly, a black swallowtail, was minutes from emerging, and the delicate pattern of the wing peeked from behind the wall of the chrysalis.

Ashlyn was ecstatic. For several weeks now, she had watched the egg grow into a caterpillar, the caterpillar into an even bigger caterpillar, and then the larger caterpillar mysteriously into the cocoon.

The back door swung open as Ashlyn's mom joined her on the porch.

"Look, Mom. The caterpillar, uh…butterfly is about come out!"

"It sure is, sweetie. You've waited a long time to see this."

"How does it do that? It was all squirmy as a caterpillar, then all stiff in the cocoon. And now a butterfly is supposed to come out of there, wings and all?"

Ashlyn's mom laughed. "It definitely is going to be a whole new creation."

Ashlyn turned around to face her mom.

"Hey, my Sunday School teacher said the same thing. Only she wasn't talking about butterflies. At least, I don't think she was."

"What do you mean?"

"Miss Carla was talking about how we all need Jesus to do something to our hearts. This act makes us a new creation so we can walk with Jesus and then be with him after we die."

"Miss Carla was right. No matter how young or old we are, our hearts without Jesus are crusty old cocoons. We need him so we can be born again—to become a new creation, just like this butterfly."

"Therefore, if anyone is in Christ, the new creation has come. The old has gone, the new is here!"

2 Corinthians 5:17

What about me?

Have you ever wondered like Ashlyn how a magnificent butterfly comes from a little old caterpillar? It's a beautiful transformation God does to the caterpillar in that cocoon. He does an even more beautiful act in your heart when you are born again. He wants to make you into new creature, one who will walk with him, one who will live with him forever. On the outside, you'll look the same, but on the inside, you'll be different. You are a new creation, because he lives in you.

Day 34: Scary Dreams

Have you ever woken up in the middle of the night from a scary dream? Maybe in the dream a monster is chasing you, you can't find your parents in a store, or you are stuck in slow-motion and can't escape from the bad guys. Scary, right? Is there anything you can do?

Even though the frightening images in your dreams seem very real, remember they are only dreams!

God doesn't want his kids to feel scared, and he's given us lots of promises that help us defeat those fearful feelings. Whenever we're feeling scared, we can pull out a scripture that shrinks our fears until they disappear. Meanwhile, our mind is protected and made stronger!

When I was little, I used to have nightmares a lot, and sometimes I couldn't sleep well. I told my mom this, and she sat down on my bed with her Bible. We wanted to find a scripture that would help me sleep better at night. We found this one:

"In peace I will lie down and sleep, for you alone, Lord, make me dwell in safety."

Psalm 4:8

I memorized this scripture, and whenever I had a hard time falling asleep or had a scary dream, I would repeat this to myself, and God would replace my fear with his peace. And his peace is awesome.

Here is another one:

"I lay down and slept, yet I woke up in

safety, for the Lord was watching over me."

Psalm 3:5

It's OK when something scares you, just remember, God doesn't want his kids to stay scared.

What about me?

Pick one of the Psalm scriptures and write it out on a little card. Memorize it so it will always be with you in your mind. You can even slip the card in your pillowcase, so when you go to sleep, you are resting on God's promises!

Day 35: I Don't Wanna!

Shaina slumped at the piano, one hand propping up her head and the other hand plinking out the scale she was supposed to be practicing.

"Shaina! No more of that attitude! You need to practice!"

Bella half-heartedly threw clothes in her closet and shoved her board games under the bed.

Her dad poked his head in the door and saw her lazy actions.

"Bella, is that how we clean our room? Let's have a good attitude now."

Have you heard your parents say phrases like this? We all have chores we don't want to do. We all have days when we don't want to go to school, don't want to go to dance class, and don't want to practice the piano.

God knows that we have to do chores that we don't like sometimes, but he also knows they are still good for us. He wants you to not only do them, but have a good attitude while you do it.

What does having a good attitude look like? It means not rolling your eyes, obeying quickly, and not complaining.

"Do everything without grumbling or

arguing."

Philippians 2:14

There it is, right in the Bible—no complaining! Even though we may hear that voice in our head saying "I don't wanna," we don't have to listen to that voice.

What about me?

Next time you're tempted to have a bad attitude, tell that bad attitude to go far away, and get out your good attitude instead.

Day 36: Scary!

Sometimes we let our imaginations get the better of us. There is a scene in the movie *Snow White and the Seven Dwarfs* when she is imagining all sorts of fearsome creatures in the forest. They turn out to be harmless rabbits and deer! Nothing like the scary monsters she was imagining.

We often let our minds imagine the worst case scenario, like thinking if you get separated from your parents at the mall or zoo, you'll be lost forever. We get so caught up in ourselves and our worries that we don't see our Savior Jesus standing right next to us. As Christians, God does not tell us that we will never have any trials. We definitely will! But through it all, God will calm our hearts, and we will be able to keep moving forward.

In the Bible, Jesus' disciples endured a scary situation. The disciples were fisherman, and they often fished at night when the fish were more active. While they were on the lake, a big storm arose and threatened to destroy their little boat.

All of a sudden, there was Jesus, walking across the water toward them!

"But He said to them, 'It is I, do not be afraid.'"

John 6:20

His name alone comforted the disciples, and they realized there was no need to be scared.

Even now, he is holding out his hand. All we have to do is reach out and take it, and he will fight for us. He has been right there all along.

What about me?

Pray this with me:

God, thank you that you protect me and take away my fear. Thank you that you give me peace in place of the fear. Thank you that you are right here with me, because that makes all the difference.

In Jesus' name, amen.

Day 37: I Just Wanna Punch Something!

Maybe your baby brother just ripped your favorite book. Maybe your best friend talked behind your back. Maybe you just found out your parents are splitting up.

You feel a bubble of anger rising up, and you're not sure what to do. The Bible talks about anger, and even Jesus got angry (check out John 2:13-21). Anger is a dangerous thing to handle—like a hot pot. You have to handle with caution. Sometimes you'll feel angry—we all feel that way from time to time. It's OK to feel angry, but don't add sin to it. Let's say you're angry because your big sister won't spend time with you, so you decide to steal some of her clothes or read her journal. Those choices would be sinning in your anger.

In your anger do not sin: "Do not let the sun go down while you are still angry."

Ephesians 4:26

Instead, find a safe way to release your anger: scream in your pillow, jog around the backyard, or pop some bubble wrap. Or you can draw a face to express your emotion, then tear it up and throw it away. Once you've cooled down, you can go back to the person you are frustrated with and make an effort to work through the conflict. Explain to them why you are feeling that way, and make a plan to avoid that situation in the future. These are healthier ways of dealing with anger.

What about me?

If you are still struggling with angry thoughts and feelings, tell a trusted adult who can help you deal with anger in a healthy way.

Day 38: Tears

When I was younger, I hated crying. It didn't happen very often that the tears overflowed my eyes, but when they did, I always felt embarrassed. It was a horrible feeling. Little did I know that God actually knows and cares about when I cry.

"...for the Lord has heard the sound of my weeping."

Psalm 6:8b

He knows if you are crying over a grandparent who died or friend who betrayed you. He knows when you're crying tears of joy over kicking the winning goal in soccer or running your best time at a track meet. Whatever the reason, whether your tears are hidden from the world or out in the open, he sees them all. And he keeps track of them.

That speaks of an incredibly intimate God. One who cares deeply for us, one who hurts with us. He doesn't tell us to stop crying like a baby or tap his foot in impatience. God instead lets us cry and comforts us.

"Trust in him at all times, O people; pour out

your heart to him, for God is our refuge."

Psalm 62:8

There is relief in knowing that God knows the depths of our hearts and doesn't push us away. He pulls us in for a big bear hug, tears and all.

What about me?

Tell God about the things that are making you sad. Don't hold anything back, but talk to him like you would a friend. Thank him for listening to you and always comforting you.

Day 39: After the Storm

Sometimes when it rains, it seems like the sky is crying, doesn't it? The downpour pounds the ground, flooding streets and trampling poor little plants. Why does the rain have to do that?

However, did you know that in order for a seed to fully grow and blossom, part of the seed has to die?

The part of the seed that pushes through the surface of the ground is hidden inside a shell that has to fall off in order for what's inside to grow into a beautiful plant.

Even if rain and storms make us sad or scared, they come to yield growth. In order for a seed to become something greater, it must go through change. Don't be afraid of tough times in your life. Instead, snuggle close to God and ask what the storm means, what he is doing in your life, and what he wants you to learn.

What about me?

God brings beauty into our lives. He will never leave something undone or unfinished. So when the rain and storms come, don't stay sad; ask God for an umbrella!

You can trust in Him.

"Weeping may stay for the night,

but rejoicing comes with the morning."

Psalm 30:5

Day 40: A Time for Everything

Change is not my favorite, but as humans, we can't escape change.

You grow up, you change schools, your friends move away, you move away, your family switches churches, loved ones die...change is all around us.

It's easy to be afraid of change. A lot of people are afraid of just that. But as children of God, we don't have to be afraid of change.

"There is a time for everything, and a season for every activity under the heavens."

Ecclesiastes 3:1

God has organized times and seasons for every type of activity. And given his track record, we can trust in his wisdom and his timing, even if it's not our own.

I know it hurts when friends move away or decide they don't want to be your friends anymore. But maybe God wants to bring a new special friend into your life, or he is calling you to make friends with someone you weren't expecting. It's tough when you're trying to make your way in a new school, but maybe God has big blessings waiting for you in this new place. It's scary if one of your parents lost a job, but maybe God has the most amazing job waiting in the wings. We can't see down the road how a change today affects tomorrow. But with God walking by our side, we can trust there is a time for everything, and we don't have to stay scared of change.

What about me?

In the space below, list some things that have changed or are changing in your life. Then ask God for help with the things that are changing.

Day 41: "I Thought You Were My Friend!"

Angela's eyes filled with tears as she stormed onto the bus. She hugged her pillow tightly to her chest as she marched to the back and sat heavily on the bench.

It was the last day of summer camp, and Angela was furious at her best friend, Layla.

The bus continued to fill with girls from the youth group, chattering and shuffling brightly colored backpacks and duffel bags over and into the seats.

Layla threw her stuff into the seat in front of Angela.

"What is your problem?" Layla asked.

"What's my problem? What's *my* problem? I thought you were my friend! I know it was you who said those things to the girls when I was out of the cabin. How could you do that to me?"

"You're such a baby. I was just kidding! Take it easy!" Layla laughed, shrugging off her friend's outburst as she put on her headphones and cranked up the music.

Tears spilled out of Angela's eyes.

"I thought you were my best friend," she said to the seat back. Layla, of course, didn't hear.

Have you ever been betrayed by a friend, whether with words or actions? It stings and hurts badly.

King David often experienced the same thing.

"With words of hatred they surround me;

they attack me without cause."

Psalm 109:3

If this happens to you, take your frustrations to God and a trusted adult, but don't lash out in anger at your friend or try and "get back." It may make you feel better for the moment, but in reality, you are just doing the same thing they did to you. Don't keep the hurtful cycle spinning.

What about me?

Has a friend hurt you like Layla did Angela? What did you do about it?

Day 42: Trapping Yourself

Whenever an animal is not where it's supposed to be, like a mouse in the house, people will often set a trap to catch the animal in order to stay safe.

But you would never set a trap for yourself, right? That would be ridiculous!

The Bible says, however, that when we are walking in fear of man, that we are setting a trap for ourselves.

"Fear of man will prove to be a snare, but

whoever trusts in the Lord is kept safe."

Proverbs 29:25

This verse is a test for us: is our fear of man (worrying about what others think about us) more than our trust in the Lord? If it is, we need to change that balance! Our trust in the Lord should outweigh trying to constantly please our friends by dressing or acting a certain way.

Don't trap yourself and forget who is your perfect protector and provider. You are living for an audience of One. And his approval is the one that matters.

What about me?

Are you more worried about what your friends at school think or what God thinks? Remember, God loves us perfectly, and his opinion is the only one that matters. Don't get too focused on other people's opinions.

Day 43: Let Us Rejoice!

Every day is a gift from God. Maybe you don't like Mondays or Wednesdays but love the weekends. No matter what the calendar says, if you wake up breathing, then it's a good day!

"This is the day which the Lord has made.

Let us rejoice and be glad in it."

Psalm 118:24 (NASB)

Whenever you are tempted to bash a day because it's not your "favorite," remember this scripture. The Lord has handmade each and every day, and it's full of blessing to enjoy and opportunities to fall more in love with Jesus. Don't miss out on what God has for you each day by complaining or only looking forward to what you consider to be a "fun" day or fun activity. Our response as daughters of the king should a grateful heart for each hour, each day, each season.

The more you practice choosing thankfulness over complaining, the easier it gets to have a great day!

What about me?

This week, write a thank you note to God for each day. It doesn't have to be a fancy note, but jot down two to three items that you are thankful for that happened each day. At the end of the week, look back over your notes and remember all that God did for you, in big and small ways. Stick them in your Bible as a reminder to be thankful for each day that comes your way.

Day 44: Happy Face

The last few days, we have been talking about negative emotions. Today, we're going to talk about a positive one: joy!

It's easy to remember to turn to God when things our lives are rough. We go running to him in prayer when we're in need, but it's just as important to run to him when we are overflowing with joy and happiness.

Even on the good days, we should turn our hearts and minds to Christ, knowing He is the one who gives the good days to us! As Christians, we don't want to have temporary amnesia where we forget God in the good times and only remember him in the bad.

Throughout the book of Psalm, there are many verses that are spilling over with joy, and focus on praising God in our hearts and with our voices.

"The Lord has done great things for us, and

we are filled with joy."

Psalm 126:3

This is one of my favorite verses, and it fills me with joy just reading it! God wants us to glorify him even when happy emotions are running through us.

What about me?

Draw a big smiley face in the space below to remind you that God has given us lots of things to be thankful for! Let's practice that this week!

Day 45: Working with Emotions

During these preteen years, you are going to experience a lot of emotions. More often than not, you may feel like a hot mess. That's normal. Because our minds can feel jumbled up during this time, it's important to take a step back and look at what is and what isn't an emotion so you can take care of your body's needs.

Hunger: Not an emotion. Hunger is your body's way of saying it needs more fuel. You need fuel to stay alert in class and to function at your very best.

Fatigue (Tiredness): Not an emotion. Fatigue is your body's way of saying it needs rest. Because of all the changes your body is going through, it may need more rest than usual.

Busyness: Not an emotion. Some seasons of life are busier than others. But don't be afraid to say no to some activities so you can be more rested and enjoy the important activities.

If you still feel blah, it can be helpful to draw a picture and write down some thoughts about what you feel. That can help you understand what's going through your mind. After that, pray and ask God to help you control those emotions.

Remember, God, not your emotions, is in the driver's seat. Learn about your emotions, express them in healthy ways, but remember they don't control you. Understanding this should empower you!

"But we have the mind of Christ."

1 Corinthians 2:16b

What about me?

Day 46: It's Not Fair!

You don't get to buy ice cream after your baseball game. You didn't get the toy you wanted for your birthday. Your brother or sister doesn't want to play with you.

What do these have in common? They are all disappointments.

Disappointments happen all the time, they are a part of life. So what do we do? We could end up feeling disappointed a lot of the time, but I don't think that's what God wants for us.

There are lots of stories in the Bible where God's kids were disappointed. Some of them stayed sad. But some of them looked for the lesson that God was teaching them. And they grew stronger because of it. Our God is a big God. And because of that, we can trust him no matter what. One of God's prophets was a man named Isaiah. God spoke through Isaiah and said this:

"For my thoughts are not your thoughts,

neither are your ways my ways, declares the

Lord. For as the heavens are higher than the

earth, so are my ways higher than your

ways, and my thoughts than your

thoughts."

Isaiah 55:8-9

Think how high the sun or the moon looks in the sky when you are playing in your backyard. That's how much bigger and better God's thoughts and plans are than ours.

What about me?

Pray this with me:

God, thank you that your ways and thoughts are higher than mine. Thank you that you know how to perfectly guide my life. Help me trust you more each day with my plans, dreams, and hopes.

In Jesus' name, amen.

Day 47: Having a Bad Day

Maybe you're just having one of those days. You're not exactly mad…or tired…or sad. Maybe you're a little bit of everything? Ugh, it's so hard to tell!

Everyone has those days, and it's especially true for girls your age. You had a fight with a friend, and now you have to miss out on a party, and now your teacher is asking you to do an assignment differently than you thought, and now you're in a bad mood.

How did that happen so quickly?

If you start feeling like this, you may find it helpful to stop and ask yourself, "Is this really a big deal?" If it's not, then it's best to stop pouting and sulking over it. You may feel like sulking is what teenagers are "supposed" to do, but it's not. Truthfully, pouting and sulking are more like the behavior of little kids!

It may be easier said than done, but you do have control over thoughts and your mood. They don't have to control you. Sometimes you have to give yourself a pep talk to snap out of a bad mood and back into a good one.

"David was greatly distressed because the men were talking of stoning him; each one

was bitter in spirit because of his sons and daughters. But David found strength in the Lord his God."

1 Samuel 30:6

David was going through a difficult time in his life but he didn't stay "greatly distressed." He stopped and encouraged himself in the Lord. Let's follow his example the next time we feel "greatly distressed" and take the time to remember God's promises to us, pray, and snap back into a better mood!

What about me?

In the space below, write out a list of three to five things that put you in a good mood. The next time you are in a bad mood, pull out that list (and the scripture above) and ask God to help you bring a smile back to your face!

Day 48: At the End of the Day

We've learned over the past several days that we can experience many emotions, sometimes in the same day! Whew! Sometimes that can be exhausting. My prayer is that when you feel these emotions that you won't let them overwhelm you or use them to hurt others, but that you would instead give them to God. That's the example we see in the psalms from King David.

King David wrote a lot of the book of Psalm, and you see him experiencing a wide range of emotions. Below are just a few of them.

Fear: "When I am afraid, I put my trust in you." (Psalm 56:3)

Sadness: "Why, my soul, are you downcast? Why so disturbed within me? Put your hope in God, for I will yet praise him, my Savior and my God." (Psalm 42:11)

Anger: "Do I not hate those who hate you, Lord, and abhor those who are in rebellion against you?" (Psalm 139:21)

Happiness: "I will praise the Lord all my life; I will sing praise to my God as long as I live." (Psalm 146:2)

What's amazing is that no matter what emotion he was experiencing, David ended each of his psalms by looking at his situation through God's eyes. If he was afraid, he knew to put his trust in

God. If he was sad, he knew God was his hope. If he was angry, he let God direct those strong feelings to a safe place. If he was joyful, he knew God was the source of those joyful feelings. David gives us a great example that we should follow each day. We have our ups and downs, but ultimately, we know that since we are children of God, God is taking care of all our needs, and we don't need to stay angry, or sad, or fearful.

What about me?

Pretend you're talking with your best friend. In the space below, write out what you've learned about emotions, like you were telling your friend.

Part 3:

Growing in God's Word

Getting Started

This third part is called "Growing in God's Word." In this section, you'll be learning more about God's amazing letter to us: the Bible. Yes, the Bible was written a long time ago by people you've never met, but that's just how amazing our God is. He knew the words he gave those Bible authors many years ago were just what they needed to hear, and they're just what you need to hear today.

God's word gives us energy for the day, truth to stand on, and purpose for our future. If we aren't reading God's word every day, it's like skipping meals! Yikes! That's not healthy for our physical bodies, and neither is it healthy for our spiritual bodies to skip our Bible meals.

So grab a snack, dig in, and let's grow in God's word!

Scripture Box

Today we are making a box to store the scriptures you will be memorizing in this next section, and any other verses you come across. Take some time to decorate your box to make it special for you, and then add your scriptures to it. Set your box out on your desk or nightstand so your verses will be ready for action!

Materials Needed

Small box that will hold 3x5 index cards
Index cards
Pen or pencil
Stickers, paint, scraps of paper, miscellaneous décor items

Decorate your box as you wish, and keep a stack of index cards and something to write with nearby so it's easy to add new verses.

Day 49: Not Your Ordinary Story

I have a confession to make. I love books...like a lot. I love to read, I love getting new books, I love talking about books, and yes, I love them so much, I wanted to write my own.

Stories let you meet new characters, travel to faraway places, and learn about history. They make your brain sharper by improving your vocabulary and memory. Books can do a lot of amazing things.

But there is one book that is far more powerful and amazing than any other book ever written.

The Bible. The Bible contains 66 books and was written by 40 authors over the span of approximately 1,500 years. The authors came from every walk of life, from fishermen and shepherds to doctors and kings. But the Bible clearly tells one unified story, one of God's love for us.

"All Scripture is God-breathed and is useful for teaching, rebuking, correcting and training in righteousness."

2 Timothy 3:16

The Bible is able to do all of this, even though it is a book, because it was God who inspired all of it. It was good for teaching and training of girls your age 50, 100, and 500 years ago because it was God who came up with it.

There are lots of people today who would say the Bible is old-fashioned, that it was just a storybook, and outdated.

But the Bible is no ordinary book, no ordinary story, because its divine author is God.

What about me?

Day 50: Living Word

Yesterday we talked about how the Bible is powerful and still good for teaching, correction, and training these many hundreds and hundreds of years after it was completed.

Not only is the Bible powerful, but it is also living. Yes, living!

"For the word of God is alive and active.

Sharper than any double-edged sword, it

penetrates even to dividing soul and spirit,

joints and marrow; it judges the thoughts

and attitudes of the heart."

Hebrews 4:12

The scriptures in the Bible don't just lie there on the page. God uses them to work in your life, sometimes even when you don't notice it!

This scripture talks about how the Bible is able to figure out tough mysteries, complicated ideas that are woven tightly together.

Does your heart ever feel confused and all mixed-up, like you don't know what's going on in there? The Bible can help you figure it out! Whatever situation you find yourself in, the Bible is there to help you figure out those tough problems. It's no ordinary story!

What about me?

As you work through this next section, it's my hope (and God's plan) that these verses come to life for you, that you begin to see them at work.

Pray this with me:

Jesus, thank you for your amazing gift of the Bible. Help these verses come to life in my own life. Help me as I memorize these scriptures, that they would help me better follow you. Even when I don't understand all that I'm reading, I trust you to give me wisdom as I study and meditate on your words.

In Jesus' name, amen.

Day 51: These Things Are Written

Have you ever wondered why God decided to write his words down in the Bible? That's a lot of words, over a long period of time, with lots of different characters in the pages.

At the end of the book of John, there is an amazing verse on why God wrote the Bible.

"But these are written so that you may believe that Jesus is the Messiah, the Son of God, and that by believing you may have life in his name."

John 20:31

The whole purpose of the Bible is so that we can get to know Jesus and come to believe in Him. By believing in Him, we have life!

Other people try to make it complicated, but I believe in keeping it simple. We have the Bible so we can believe in Jesus, then share with others so they can believe. What an amazing book the Bible is!

What about me?

Do you believe yet? If God and you have been talking, and you know that he is what's missing in your life, today would be a great day to give your life to Him!

Pray this with me:

Jesus, I know I've messed up and can't do this on my own. I believe you died for my sins and rose again and want to give me eternal life. I believe and receive that gift! Come into my heart and help learn about you and follow you.

In Jesus' name, amen.

Day 52: Truer than True

We've seen how God's word is living and powerful, and we've seen how the Bible is his special message to us. The words are intended to change whoever comes into contact with them.

God's word is also true. Not just true, but truer than true. It's the definition of truth. There is no lie or deception in it.

"The Word became flesh and made his dwelling among us. We have seen his glory, the glory of the one and only Son, who came from the Father, full of grace and truth."

John 1:14

From the beginning of the Church, people outside the Church have tried to attack the word of God. They try to say it isn't true, they try to add parts or take away parts, and they try to diminish its value.

But God's word has stood the test of time. We can depend on it. We can believe it. God isn't going to lead us astray or try to fool us. He's not into playing jokes on us. We can believe and know that his word is true.

What about me?

Day 53: Don't Be a Chameleon

A chameleon is a type of lizard that has a secret set of skills. Do you know what it is?

Chameleons can blend into any sort of surroundings or backgrounds as a way to keep them safe from predators as a part of their survival skills.

Even though God gave this ability to one of his animal creations, he does not want his children to practice this skill. In fact, he wants us to do quite the opposite!

"Do not conform to the pattern of this world, but be transformed by the renewing of your mind. Then you will be able to test and approve what God's will is—his good, pleasing and perfect will."

Romans 12:2

Do not conform any longer…God is saying we should not look like the world or try to be like the world in any way. We should stand out!

How we do we do this? Our clue is in the next part of the scripture.

"But be transformed by the renewing of your mind…" Even after we become children of God, we still need to continually update our minds to be more like God. Just like a software update for your phone fixes bugs and makes it run better, "updating" or renewing our minds every day to be more like God fixes bugs and helps our lives be better.

What about me?

A perfect way to start renewing your mind is by hiding God's word in your heart. We will be digging into this during the next several days and memorizing some powerful scriptures to help renew your mind.

Day 54: Amazing Brains

How many songs can you sing along to right now? Go ahead and list some below.

While you're at it, how many family birthdays can you remember?

Who are the members of your favorite band?

How fast can you text?

We are constantly taking in new information and storing it away for future use. Our brains are amazing machines!

Now how many scriptures do you know by heart? List just the reference of each scripture.

Sometimes we think memorizing scriptures is really hard and that we can't do it. But we can! Like you've just shown here, you already have so much information stored in your brain and can process information rapidly. You just have to create a new habit of memorizing scripture!

"I have hidden your word in my heart, that I might not sin against you."

Psalm 119:11

This is another great scripture to add to your collection. It keeps us focused on a big reason to memorize scripture. Scripture helps us know the right choices to make, and the wrong ones to avoid.

What about me?

Write out today's scripture on an index card and begin working on memorizing it. How do you do that? Read it lots of times, place it somewhere where you will see it throughout the day, and even have your friends or family quiz you on it. While you may not be able to memorize all of these scriptures just yet, I would encourage you to start somewhere. When you memorize this verse, add it to your special scripture box!

Day 55: Smooth Path

Sometimes on road trips, I wait to put on the rest of my makeup as I get closer to my destination (only if someone else is driving of course). It's annoying though when I'm trying to apply eyeliner or mascara, and the car hits a bumpy patch of road. Watch out! It's so hard to apply a smooth line of eyeliner when the car is vibrating and my hand is shaking.

Bumpy roads do us no good. In fact, God has something to say about it.

"Make level paths for your feet, so that the lame may not be disabled, but rather healed."

Hebrews 12:13

There should be a smooth a path from our hearts to God's heart, like a newly-paved road.

If there are ruts and potholes on our heart paths, they make it harder to focus on God and hear his message, just like it makes it harder to apply makeup in a bumpy car. It's not a smooth trip.

Maybe it's a rut of a bad attitude, disobedience, lying, or cheating. Maybe you've made a habit of being mean to your younger sibling or pestering your older sibling.

Whatever those ruts are, they need to be filled in, and one of the ways to do this is by memorizing scripture. No matter if those ruts have been there three days, three weeks, or three years, we must make straight paths for our hearts and minds.

What about me?

Write out today's scripture on an index card and begin working on memorizing it. How do you do that? read it lots of times, place it somewhere where you will see it throughout the day, and even have your friends or family quiz you on it. We're just getting started! Hang in there, my friend!

Day 56: Sweeter than Honey

One of my favorite breakfasts is peanut butter toast with honey. The peanut butter fills me up, and that honey is so sweet on my tongue!

In the book of Psalm, there are a couple of verses that talk about scriptures being sweeter to our mouths than honey. Do we love God's word that much? Do we think it's even sweeter than our favorite sugary treat?

I love sweet treats as much (if not more) than the next person. But desserts only taste good for a little while. And they are really not good for our bodies.

God's word is different. God's word makes our life sweet and wonderful and is always good for us!

"The decrees of the Lord are firm, and all of them are righteous. They are more precious than gold, than much pure gold; they are sweeter than honey, than honey from the honeycomb."

Psalm 19:9b-10

"How sweet are your words to my taste,

sweeter than honey to my mouth!"

Psalm 119:103

What about me?

As you memorize one of these verses from Psalm, how can you practice desiring God's word more than your favorite sugary treat?

Day 57: In One Ear, Out the Other

When I was in elementary school, there was a Bible show on early Saturday mornings called *The Gospel Bill Show*. They would play short cartoons in between segments of the show. One in particular I still remember; the cartoon was about building your house on the rock, the rock of God's Word.

There was a strong castle built by the ocean, and no matter how hard the waves beat against the walls, the castle stood firm. A later clip showed a flimsy sandcastle, and as soon as a wave beat against it, it crumbled and dissolved back into the ocean.

"Therefore everyone who hears these words of mine and puts them into practice is like a wise man who built his house on the rock. The rain came down, the streams rose, and the winds blew and beat against that house; yet it did not fall, because it had its foundation on the rock."

Matthew 7:24-25

As we've been talking about hiding God's word in our hearts, it's not enough just to know it, or even just to memorize it. We have to *do* what it says. If we don't, we are no better than a sandcastle that will just be claimed by the ocean again, or a Lego house that can easily be knocked down.

By not only hiding God's word in our hearts, but also doing what it says, we are building a firm place to stand on throughout our lives.

I love visiting the beach, but every time, I'm amazed at how fickle the sands are; dangerous even. You can't depend on it to stay in the same place or support you. But you can depend on the word of God. Don't let it go in one ear, then out the other. Listen and obey.

What about me?

Write out today's scripture on an index card and begin working on memorizing it by reading it lots of times, placing it somewhere where you will see it throughout the day, and even by having your friends or family quiz you on scripture.

Day 58: Powerful Thoughts

"Watch your thoughts, for they become your words.
Watch your words, for they become your actions.
Watch your actions, for they become your habits.
Watch your habits, for they become your character.
Watch your character, for that becomes your destiny."
-Author Unknown

I first read this popular saying in elementary school, and it has stuck with me ever since. Sometimes we think little old thoughts aren't that powerful. They're just little old thoughts, and they're hidden inside our brain. What harm can they cause?

Thoughts have a way of setting off a chain reaction, for good or for bad. It's kind of like setting up dominoes in a fancy pattern and then knocking them all down. Thoughts influence the words you speak, which influence how you act throughout the day, and ultimately how people come to know you.

In Philippians 4, we find some guidelines on what we should think about:

"Finally, brothers and sisters, whatever is

true, whatever is noble, whatever is right,

whatever is pure, whatever is lovely,

whatever is admirable—if anything is

excellent or praiseworthy—think about such

things."

Philippians 4:8

If you hold up your thoughts to this standard, and they meet this standard, then thumbs up! They are good thoughts that will lead you in a good direction.

But if a thought doesn't meet this standard, toss it in the trash and think a God thought!

What about me?

Write out today's scripture on an index card and begin working on memorizing it by reading it lots of times, placing it somewhere where you will see it throughout the day, and even by having your friends or family quiz you on scripture.

Day 59: Even When You're Young

My biggest goal when I was young was to be grown up. Grownups seemed to have all the fun, and I couldn't wait to be in that group.

Two of my specific goals were to drink a whole can of Coke (since my mom only let me drink part of one) and to stay up late. Now that I can be considered a "grownup," I usually choose to drink tea instead of Coke, and I like going to bed on time!

While it's fun to dream about what you'll get to do when you're older, don't forget how important *now* is. There are still important things to do when you're young. Jesus speaks to those youngest believers in verses like this one:

"Don't let anyone look down on

you because you are young, but set an

example for the believers in speech, in

conduct, in love, in faith and in purity."

1 Timothy 4:12

There is no reason to think that you have to wait to live for Christ as an adult; you can start right now.

In the first scripture, it's says that young believers can set an example for other believers. Other people are always watching, and you would be surprised to find out how much your actions could influence someone else.

One of the earliest scriptures I remember memorizing says that even a kid builds a reputation by his actions (Proverbs 20:11 KJV). One of the ways you can start living for God right now and setting an example for all believers is to tuck these verses away in your mind and your heart so you'll always have them.

Trust me, it *is* fun to be young!

What about me?

Write out today's scripture on an index card and begin working on memorizing it by reading it lots of times, placing it somewhere where you will see it throughout the day, and even by having your friends or family quiz you on scripture. These are great verses to encourage you. Don't skip them, just take your time as you memorize them.

Day 60: So Thirsty!

After a long bike ride or run, I can't wait to gulp down some water or a sports drink. Or if I've been doing yard work on a hot summer afternoon, I can't wait to get a snow cone or slushie. It's all I can think about!

Did you know that the Bible calls Jesus the Living Water? What does that even mean?

Even if I gulp down a sports drink or enjoy a slushie, it will only satisfy my thirst for a little bit. Eventually, I'll need something else to drink. And eventually, I'll be craving another slushie. They only satisfy for a little while. Jesus provides a different kind of satisfaction, one that lasts forever. That's right, *forever.*

We can come and get our fill and know that Jesus will never leave us feeling thirsty.

The Bible also speaks of thirsting after him and his word. Just like our physical bodies were made to consume a lot of water, our spirits were made to thirst after Jesus and consume his living water.

"You, God, are my God, earnestly I seek you;

I thirst for you, my whole being longs for

you, in a dry and parched land where there

is no water."

Psalm 63:1

What about me?

The next time you're thirsty, think about how God satisfies our thirst like nothing else ever can. He is the slushie that never ends!

Day 61: Resist

Does this sound familiar to you? We know what God wants us to do, but sometimes it's just so hard to do it. It feels like we are being pulled away from what we know is right, toward what we know is wrong.

We know we should obey our parents cheerfully, but we don't want to do that.

We know we should study for that test, but it would be so easy to peek at someone else's paper.

We know we should be nice and play with our young sibling, but we'd rather shut the door to our room.

That's called temptation. Temptation occurs when the enemy tries to trick us into thinking that he knows best or when we believe that we know best.

But that's not true! God always tells the truth and always knows what's best. The enemy is incapable of telling the truth.

So what are we to do when temptation comes? We know it's coming; even Jesus was tempted! (Check out Matthew 4).

Resisting temptation starts with bending your knee, and with acknowledging that God does know best and that you need his help.

"Submit yourselves, then, to God. Resist the devil, and he will flee from you."

James 4:7

Fleeing temptation starts with submitting to God. The enemy doesn't stand a chance against that! And that's what Jesus did, too. When the enemy came to tempt Him, Jesus put himself under the authority of God by repeating what God had said. And it worked. The enemy had to flee.

What about me?

Write out today's scripture on an index card and begin working on memorizing it by reading it lots of times, placing it somewhere where you will see it throughout the day, and even by having your friends or family quiz you on scripture. This is a great fighting verse! Tuck it away so you always have it to pull out when the enemy tempts you!

Day 62: You Can Stay, You Have to Go

Our brain is very powerful and complex. It's incredible to think about all the detail God put into creating our brains! For example:

- Your brain puts off enough electricity to power a small light bulb.
- The brain sends more electrical signals in a day than all the phone messages in the world. Imagine all those texts and Snapchats!
- Signals between your brain and body move at speeds more than 150 mph.

Thoughts come and go through our brain; some are good thoughts and some are bad thoughts. Good thoughts get to stay and grow in our garden. Bad thoughts are weeds, and they have to be pulled out immediately and thrown away.

God has given us the ability to control our thoughts and only let good ones bloom in our gardens.

"We demolish arguments and every

pretension that sets itself up against the

knowledge of God, and we take captive

every thought to make it obedient to

Christ."

2 Corinthians 10:5

Through prayer and God's help, you have the ability to be in charge of your thoughts! Thoughts do not control the children of God; we control our thoughts. Just like this scripture says, we take them captive, like an intruder in our camp.

It's not about being perfect, but with practice, we will become quick to identify good thoughts and bad thoughts alike. And know you know what to say to bad thoughts: Take a hike!

What about me?

Write out today's scripture on an index card and begin working on memorizing it by reading it lots of times, placing it somewhere where you will see it throughout the day, and even by having your friends or family quiz you on scripture. While you may not be able to memorize all of these scriptures just yet, getting started is half the battle.

Day 63: 3:16

We've spent some time hiding away powerful parts of God's Word in our hearts, and there's still so much more out there! We will never run out of scriptures to memorize!

Perhaps the most important verse you can memorize, if you haven't already, is John 3:16.

"For God so loved the world that he gave his one and only Son, that whoever believes in him should not perish but have eternal life."

John 3:16

The whole gospel, the whole Bible, really, is summed up in this one verse. It has the power to change lives, to deliver truth, and to reveal Christ.

That's one power-packed verse!

This tells us, first of all, that God loves us. So much in fact, that his only Son came to live on earth with the purpose of taking our punishment, even though he did nothing wrong. It then tells us the good news, that all we need to do is believe in order to receive the gift of eternal life!

John 3:16 is loved all over the world, and rightly so. It brightens the world like the sun coming out from behind the clouds after a storm. It comforts the heart like a loved one's hug. It's the best news you'll ever hear!

What about me?

Write out today's scripture on an index card and begin working on memorizing it by reading it lots of times, placing it somewhere where you will see it throughout the day, and even by having your friends or family quiz you on scripture. You'll also have this verse stored away to share with your friends who may not know Jesus yet.

Day 64: Did You Know?

There are a total of 66 books in the Bible, 39 in the Old Testament and 27 in the New Testament.

The shortest verse in the Bible contains only two words: "*Jesus wept.*" (John 11:35).

The longest verse in the Bible contains 90 words: "*Then were the king's scribes called at that time in the third month, that is, the month Sivan, on the three and twentieth day thereof; and it was written according to all that Mordecai commanded unto the Jews, and to the lieutenants, and the deputies and rulers of the provinces which are from India unto Ethiopia, an hundred twenty and seven provinces, unto every province according to the writing thereof, and unto every people after their language, and to the Jews according to their writing, and according to their language.*" (Esther 8:9).

More than 40 authors contributed to the writing of the Bible.

The Bible was written in three languages: Hebrew, Aramaic, and Greek. It was written on three continents: Asia, Africa, and Europe

The Bible was written over a 1,500-year span (from 1400 B.C to A.D. 100) over 40 generations.

The Bible was the first book to be printed, in the year 1454 to be exact.

The Bible has been translated into more than 1,000 languages.

The longest word in the Bible happens to be the name *Maher-shalal-hash-baz*. It's found in Isaiah 8:1, and it means "quick to the plunder, swift to the spoil."

The verse in the exact middle of the Bible is Psalm 117:8. There are 594 chapters before Psalm 117 and 594 chapters after Psalm 117.

"Open my eyes that I may see wonderful things in your law."

Psalm 119:18

What About Me?

All of these authors, places, words and letters came together by God's direction to create the most beautiful, powerful book ever written. What is God saying to you through his word? Pray and ask that he opens your eyes to reveal wonderful things in his word.

Day 65: Before a Fall

Have you heard the familiar saying, "Pride goes before a fall"? This is famous saying is actually from the Bible, and it's found in the book of Proverbs.

"Pride goes before destruction, a haughty spirit before a fall."

Proverbs 16:18

What exactly does this mean? As humans, it's easy to get puffed up, feeling a little too proud about our accomplishments, our skills, and our talents. We think we're hot stuff. We think everyone is looking at us. We think we have it all together.

Oftentimes this kind of attitude is followed by some humbling event. Our eyes are so lifted up, we don't see the path before us and trip easily. Keep your eyes on the road and stay humble.

Choose humility.

What about me?

Write out today's scripture on an index card and begin working on memorizing it by reading it lots of times, placing it somewhere where you will see it throughout the day, and even by having your friends or family quiz you on scripture.

Day 66: The Right Kind of Fear

Usually the Bible talks about fear in a bad way, in a way that we should avoid or get rid of it. Angels tell humans "Do not fear." God tells us that "perfect love casts out fear," and also that we do not have "the spirit of fear."

However, there is one type of fear that the Bible says we should have. The fear of the Lord. What? He's our Father and savior, right? Why should we be afraid of him?

Let's look at a different definition of fear:

"To have a reverential awe of; to have a feeling of respect and wonder for something very powerful" (Merriam-Webster).

Do you have an attitude of respect and wonder for God? Or do you treat him like he's "normal"? God is anything BUT normal. He knows all. He sees all. He is God.

"And now, Israel, what does the Lord your

God ask of you but to fear the Lord your

God, to walk in obedience to him, to love

him, to serve the Lord your God with all your

heart and with all your soul..."

Deuteronomy 10:12

What about me?

Write out today's scripture on an index card and begin working on memorizing it by reading it lots of times, placing it somewhere where you will see it throughout the day, and even by having your friends or family quiz you on scripture. You can do it!

Day 67: All About Jesus

The Bible is a big book with lots of characters, towns with funny names, songs, history, and prophecy. There's lots of talk about sacrifice and animals, instructions, angels, and battles.

A lot happens between Genesis and Revelation.

Do you sometimes think you'll never understand the Bible, that there's just too much to learn? That it all seems disconnected, and it doesn't make sense? It's true that you could study the Bible your whole life and there would still be more to learn, but it may help to see that the Bible really only has one theme. It has one central figure. Jesus.

The whole Bible is about Jesus. We see throughout the pages forerunners of Jesus, and then we see Jesus as the perfect completion of these characters. He is the perfect Adam, who never sinned. He is our eternal priest, who never dies. He is the perfect Boaz, our redeemer. He is the perfect king, who was never corrupted.

As you read through the books of the Bible, look for fingerprints of Jesus. There are hints and shadows of him from Genesis to Malachi. Then we finally get to meet him in Matthew through John. Then he leaves us his words through the Holy Spirit from Acts to Revelation.

Sure there are lots of people and stories, parables and songs. But they all point to the same thing: Jesus.

"And he is the head of the body, the church; he is the beginning and the firstborn from among the dead, so that in everything he might have the supremacy. For God was pleased to have all his fullness dwell in him, and through him to reconcile to himself all things, whether things on earth or things in heaven, by making peace through his blood, shed on the cross."

Colossians 1:18-20

What about me?

Day 68: Laughing at the Future

As a child of God, we have so much to look forward to. Not only can we trust in the fact that God is taking care of us in this life, we get to spend eternity with Him! We have important purposes to fulfill in this life, and we will have important purposes to fulfill in the life to come.

The Bible assures us that God has good plans in store for us, plans to prosper us and not to harms us (Jeremiah 29:11). We can look forward with excitement toward the future. One of my favorite verses about the future comes from Proverbs 31:

"She is clothed with strength and dignity;

she can laugh at the days to come."

Proverbs 31:25

I love the confidence in this verse. God doesn't want us to be scared, timid little girls. God has clothed us with his strength and dignity (honor), and he wants us to look forward to the future and what we are growing into. I just love this promise from God.

What about me?

Write out today's scripture on an index card and begin working on memorizing it by reading it lots of times, placing it somewhere where you will see it throughout the day, and even by having your friends or family quiz you on scripture. Look at far you've come already!

Day 69: Not Ashamed

If you are proud of something, you're going to talk about it, right? Let's say you won an award at school or scored the winning goal in your soccer game or achieved something else? You're probably going to tell everyone who comes across your path about it. Or at the very least, your parents will tell everyone!

Or maybe you have a special item that's been in your family for a while, like a vase, a book or a quilt. I'm sure you or your parents take very good care of it. You tell people about it, display it, and for sure don't hide it away.

We have received the greatest gift we could ever receive in the gift of salvation. We should be proud of it, talk about it, and display it where everyone can see it.

"For I am not ashamed of the

gospel, because it is the power of God that

brings salvation to everyone who believes..."

Romans 1:16a

We shouldn't be ashamed of the gospel. Yes, maybe it feels awkward sometimes talking about it, but remember how powerful it is! Remember how much it cost Jesus!

If we treasure something, if we are proud of it, we shouldn't be ashamed of it. We shouldn't hide it. The gospel is no different.

What about me?

Write out today's scripture on an index card and begin working on memorizing it by reading it lots of times, placing it somewhere where you will see it throughout the day, and even by having your friends or family quiz you on scripture. Be patient with yourself if it seems like it's taking a while to memorize a scripture. Stick with it, and soon it will stick to your mind.

Day 70: Better Than You?

It starts out simple. Maybe you have a new outfit you're really excited about—like really proud of. Or you get to have a birthday party in a really cool place.

You might think, *Wow this is so neat! I am so glad this is happening to me. I am so awesome! I bet everyone wishes they could have a party like this! I bet everyone wishes they could look like me.*

These are dangerous thoughts. What does God's word have to say about how we view ourselves and each other?

"Be devoted to one another in love. Honor one another above yourselves. Live in harmony with one another. Do not be proud...Do not be conceited."

Romans 12:10, 16

Honor one another above yourself…don't choose pride.

You'll never win if you constantly compare yourself to others. God will take care of you. You don't have to elevate yourself. Honor others, and God will take care of your end. You can't go wrong with that path.

What about me?

Write out today's scripture on an index card and begin working on memorizing it by reading it lots of times, placing it somewhere where you will see it throughout the day, and even by having your friends or family quiz you on scripture. You are doing an awesome job!

Day 71: Shining Like Stars

"Do everything without grumbling or arguing, so that you may become blameless and pure, 'children of God without fault in a warped and crooked generation.' Then you will shine among them like stars in the sky."

Philippians 2:14-15

I love the last part of that verse above...shine like stars in the sky. How majestic! How beautiful! I want to be like that!

But how do you get to be like stars in the sky? The answer is in the first part of the verse. No grumbling. No complaining. No arguing.

Ouch...guilty!

We've all complained or argued at some point. Maybe it seems like no big deal. Everyone does it, right?

To God, it is a big deal. The next time you're tempted to complain about cleaning your room, taking out the trash, or visiting a neighbor, think about this verse and zip the lips. Stop the complaint before it starts, and you will shine like a star.

What about me?

Write out today's scripture on an index card and begin working on memorizing it by reading it lots of times, placing it somewhere where you will see it throughout the day, and even by having your friends or family quiz you on scripture.

Day 72: Perfect Protection

There are many verses throughout the Bible that tell of God promising protection to his children.

"Let the beloved of the Lord rest secure in him, for he shields him all day long, and the one the Lord loves rests between his shoulders."

Deuteronomy 33:12

"He is my loving God and my fortress, my stronghold and my deliverer, my shield, in whom I take refuge..."

Psalm 144:2

These are just two of them. During storms or when I have to stay at our house by myself, I remind myself of these scriptures. God provides the perfect protection, better than any human can offer.

When scary situations arise, it's important you uproot fearful thoughts quickly and replant with the promises of God. When you uproot quickly, the thoughts won't have time to bear ugly fruit.

The God of the universe is the best security system I can think of!

What about me?

Write out one of today's scripture on an index card and begin working on memorizing it by reading it lots of times, placing it somewhere where you will see it throughout the day, and even by having your friends or family quiz you on scripture.

Day 73: Let Your Words Be Few

One day in junior high, I became convinced that my work as a student was *way* harder than the job my mom had, as a mother and my teacher. She was both to me because she homeschooled my brother and I.

I was sure that she didn't understand how hard my schoolwork was and how much I had to do. I was sure I knew better.

She agreed to "switch places" for the day. She had to do my homework and a few chores, but I had to grade her (my) work, do laundry, do the dishes, and get dinner ready.

It was the longest day of my life. My mom's job was way harder! My perspective changed, and I realized I had it pretty good as a kid and student.

We must be careful to not get the same attitude with God. It might be tempting to think that God doesn't understand what we are going through. But God is God. He does know what we are going through, as well as what all his other kids are going through.

"Do not be quick with your mouth, do not

be hasty in your heart to utter anything

before God. God is in heaven and you are on

earth, so let your words be few."

Ecclesiastes 5:2

I was rash with my words, thinking my job was harder than my mom's. In reality, I didn't know what I was talking about!

Remember God is in heaven, and we are just on earth. Let's guard against having a big mouth!

What about me?

Write out today's scripture on an index card and begin working on memorizing it by reading it lots of times, placing it somewhere where you will see it throughout the day, and even by having your friends or family quiz you on scripture.

Day 74: Freedom

"Then you will know the truth, and the truth will set you free."

John 8:32

Did you know that God desires you to be free? Free to follow him courageously, free to live victoriously, and free to love others generously? Free from guilt, free from fear. That's what he wants for your life. How amazing is that?

The enemy, on the other hand, does not want you to be free. He doesn't want you to know about your freedom. He wants you to be trapped by guilt and fear. He wants you to be fearful of loving and giving. He will do everything he can to keep you trapped.

The truth is what sets us free, but lies trap us. Anytime you think a lie is your escape, your way out, it's a trick. Just like cheese on a mousetrap, it looks good for a moment, but lies will only trap us more.

Truth sets us free! Choose truth today!

What about me?

Write out today's scripture on an index card and begin working on memorizing it by reading it lots of times, placing it somewhere where you will see it throughout the day, and even by having your friends or family quiz you on scripture. This is such a powerful verse! I'm proud of you for memorizing it!

Day 75: Your Future

Did you know that God has a purpose for you? Do you think that his purpose for you are good or bad? You can trust God's purposes for you are always for the best.

"'For I know the plans I have for you,' declares the Lord, 'plans to prosper you and not to harm you, plans to give you hope and a future.'"

Jeremiah 29:11

Even though we can't see the future, we belong to the one who can. Maybe your mind is full of "What if" questions? Maybe you are facing a scary future right now, like your parents divorcing, an illness, or a move to another town. Or maybe life is pretty normal right now. That's the cool thing about God's plans. No matter what your life is like in this moment, God's heart toward you will never change. He is always planning hope and good things for us. The road to get there may not look like what we were expecting, but again, that's where faith and trust come in.

We can trust that our future is safe with God, even when the "What if's" seem scary.

What about me?

Write out today's scripture on an index card and begin working on memorizing it by reading it lots of times, placing it somewhere where you will see it throughout the day, and even by having your friends or family quiz you on scripture. I still repeat this one to myself all the time. It's one of my favorite verses!

Day 76: Like a Tiny Seed

What is the tiniest thing you can imagine? A tiny jewel? A speck of dust? A grain of salt? How about a mustard seed?

Huh?

Those tiny black dots pictured above are mustard seeds. And there is even a special scripture about those seeds in the Bible.

Truly I tell you, if you have faith as small as a mustard seed, you can say to this mountain, 'Move from here to there,' and it will move. Nothing will be impossible for you."

Matthew 17:20

Maybe it feels like you don't know much about your faith or can't do much with it. Maybe you feel like your faith is not very strong. Maybe it seems you have to wait until you're older to really accomplish something for God.

God wants you to exercise your faith right now, no matter how small you think it is. Look at those tiny seeds again. That's all it takes for God to work through you.

What about me?

What do you need to have faith for in your life? Doing well in school? Reaching your lost friends? Maybe a family member or pet is sick, or maybe you are nervous about an upcoming audition or tryout. Whatever is, stand on your mustard-seed faith, and see all that God will do!

Part 4:

Growing in Prayer

Getting Started

This last part is called "Growing in Prayer." In this section, you'll be learning about how to listen to God and tell him what's on your heart. Sure, prayer seems hard at first, since we can't see God. But prayer is so important to growing in our faith. He wants to hear what's on our hearts. He wants to tell us truth and give us direction. So we pray.

We'll start slow, but by the end of the section (and actually, it's the end of the book, *sniff*) you'll be more confident in your prayer life.

Ready to get started? Let's do this!

Day 77: How Do You Know?

Do you ever wonder how people know stuff? Especially adults. Like, how do they know so much?

I remember being a kid and wanting to be an adult so bad. I wanted to *know* things and get to do all the cool stuff that, you know, adults get to do.

A lot of knowledge and wisdom comes with age. The longer you've been around, the more you will know. But since we are children of God, he gives extra help in the wisdom department. How does that work?

"The fear of the Lord is the beginning of knowledge, but fools despise wisdom and instruction."

Proverbs 1:7

It can't get simpler than that! Knowledge and wisdom starts with the fear of the Lord. Fearing the Lord puts us in the right place before him, humbling ourselves to receive the wisdom we need.

The fear of the Lord is our starting place.

What about me?

Day 78: What is Prayer?

Think about the last conversation you had with your mom or your grandpa or your best friend. I'm guessing both of you took turns talking and listening. There might have been serious parts to your conversation, maybe some funny parts.

I'm also hoping you gave whoever you were talking to your full attention and didn't answer a call or start picking your nose or something.

Prayer is a conversation between you and God. Both of you will talk, and God is always listening. It's us who need practice listening. The Bible talks a lot about prayer, but you still may be a little confused as to where to start.

For starters, you don't have to have a lot of words, and you definitely don't have to use fancy words. Check out Matthew 6:7. You also don't have to pray in the same place or even at the same time every day. God knows that prayer keeps us connected to him, so he wants us to learn to pray so that we keep our hearts turned toward him

In the rest of Matthew 6, we find some more guidelines for prayer in "The Lord's Prayer."

"Our Father in heaven, hallowed be the name." We start off by acknowledging who God is and his power.

"Your kingdom come, your will be done, on earth as it is in heaven." We also acknowledge that it's his plan that will prevail.

"Give us today our daily bread." We ask him to meet our needs.

"Forgive us our debts, as we also have forgiven our debtors." Here we ask for forgiveness while also practicing forgiveness with those in our lives.

"And lead us not into temptation, but deliver us from the evil one." And we ask for his help in resisting temptations.

What about me?

This gives us a template for prayer, a starting place. As you learn and grow, so will your prayers, but you have to start somewhere. I would encourage you to memorize the Lord's Prayer as a guideline to help build your prayer life.

Day 79: Ask, Seek, Knock

I remember when I first started praying regularly on my own. I was almost ten, and my grandpa was in the hospital. I remember being prompted that I should pray for him, and as I began to do that, the Lord brought other people to mind that needed prayer.

That prayer has evolved and changed over the years, but it's now my habit to begin and end each day with prayer, with lots of little prayers in between.

Prayer journals are also an important part of my prayer life. I started journaling when my cousin gave me a journal one Christmas. Recorded throughout my journals are prayers and struggles I've walked through, and whenever God answers a prayer, I make sure to record what happened.

Seeing years of answered prayer is always such an encouragement to me. We serve a faithful God! He is ready and waiting to listen to us and to answer our prayers.

"Ask, and it will be given to you; seek, and you will find; knock, and it will be opened to you. For everyone who asks receives, and the one who seeks finds, and to the one

who knocks it will be opened."

Matthew 7: 7-8

What about me?

Keep in mind this isn't about making a wish list and sending it up to God. As you spend more time with him, you begin to desire what he wants, so your prayers will line up with his will more and more. List below some prayer needs you have. Check back periodically to see how God answers them.

Day 80: God's Phone Number

Prayer is our connection to God. Just like you text or tweet a friend or FaceTime your grandma, the phone, tablet and computer are ways to connect to other people.

Even though we can't see prayer, turn on notifications, or choose a ringtone, it's an even more active and powerful communication tool to talk to God than any phone in our pocket or purse.

"Then you will call on me and come and pray to me, and I will listen to you. You will seek me and find me, when you seek me with all your heart. I will be found by you, declares the Lord..."

Jeremiah 29:12-14a

God isn't trying to hide from us or ignore our calls. He doesn't hit "Decline" when we start talking to him. He promises right here in this verse that we will find him. Connecting to God through prayer takes practice, just like any other skill. And that's OK. It's worth it.

What about me?

Pray this with me:

Dear Jesus, thank you for making a way that I can talk to you. Help me as I learn to use this tool. Help my heart to be open to what you have to say and my ears to get better at hearing your voice. I love you. Thank you for loving me.

In Jesus' name, amen.

Day 81: Secret Weapon

God has given his children many tools to grow in their faith and grow in their knowledge of him. We read the Bible, learn from other believers, and go to church as some of the amazing tools we use.

But perhaps the most powerful, the most special tool available to us is prayer. You could even call it our secret weapon against the enemy. Prayer is our direct lifeline to God, and not only do we learn to hear his voice through it, but prayer grows our faith as well.

"Therefore confess your sins to each other and pray for each other so that you may be healed. The prayer of a righteous person is powerful and effective."

James 5:16

The prayer of a righteous person is powerful…effective. Every time I read that, I am encouraged that my time spent talking with and listening to God is worth it.

What about me?

Prayer reminds us of who we are and who we are serving, two facts that make us strong against the attacks of the enemy. The enemy wants us to forget who we are and who we serve. That's why it's so important to keep talking to God. In the good times and not so good times, keep your prayer weapon sharp and ready to use at a moment's notice.

Day 82: All Things

When I was about ten years old, I was preparing to go to my very first dance competition. The dance I was in was a production number, so that means a dance with a lot of people in it, and the song was five or six minutes long.

We were rehearsing a few weeks before the competition, and the rehearsal was going a little rough. I began to feel inadequate and was afraid I was going to mess up the dance.

We had a lunch break, and as my dad drove me to get food, I repeated one of my favorite scriptures over and over.

"I can do all things through Christ (who)

strengthens me."

Philippians 4:13 KJV

God's word said that he would help me do all things, and I was counting on the fact that "all things" would include my very first dance competition.

And you know what? It did. We did great, and I felt God's presence and comfort.

Whether it's getting ready for a band or orchestra concert, a dance recital, your first softball game, or a science fair, God is ready and able to help you face whatever your day brings. No event or task is too small for him.

What about me?

Praying this scripture and similar ones takes our minds off our fear, off our situation, and focuses us on God. We should always have our eyes on God. He stands ready to help us with all things.

Day 83: Never Give Up

"Then Jesus told his disciples a parable to show them that they should always pray and not give up. He said: "In a certain town there was a judge who neither feared God nor cared what people thought. And there was a widow in that town who kept coming to him with the plea, 'Grant me justice against my adversary.' For some time he refused. But finally he said to himself, 'Even though I don't fear God or care what people think, yet because this widow keeps bothering me, I will see that she gets justice...'"

Luke 18:1-5

I'm not sure what challenges are facing you today, but my prayer for you is that this story is an encouragement and a challenge to not give up in prayer. Unlike the ruler in the story, God loves us deeply and is always going to take care of us. He knows our faith will grow strong when we persist in prayer.

Maybe everything is great in your life and you're enjoying a time in between storms when the sea is smooth and calm. Let this story be a seed that you plant in the garden of your heart, so that when storms do come, this verse can bloom, and you can remember to keep praying, keep praying, keep praying.

But even if everything is not OK, the lesson here is to also keep praying.

What about me?

If you're in a storm right now, think of this verse as a lifesaver that lifeguards use when they rescue people in the pool or ocean. Grab onto it, and don't let go. God hears your prayers. Keep praying, keep praying.

Day 84: The One Who Has the Answers

Sometimes your friends can be good resources when you have questions about schoolwork... sometimes. I mean, they are right there learning the same stuff you are, so it's not likely they're big experts in math or Spanish. They probably only know as much as you do. Because of that, maybe it's not a good idea to go to them when you have complicated questions about your homework.

The same is true outside of school. Sure, your friends can offer some wisdom if you have a problem, but it's important to understand that their wisdom is limited. They are right there learning about life at the same time as you, so they probably don't have a ton of experience and knowledge.

So who is the best person to go to? Adults are always a better choice than your friends. They have already walked down the path you're on and can offer better advice and help.

Going to God in prayer is also another wise choice. God knows everything. His word promises that if we ask for wisdom, he will give it to us.

"If any of you lacks wisdom, you should ask
God, who gives generously to all without
finding fault, and it will be given to you."

James 1:5

What about me?

Do you have some big questions in your life right now that you just don't know the answers to? Have you tried bringing them before the Lord? Stop and do that right now, and ask for wisdom from the one who holds all the answers.

Day 85: Jesus Prays For Us

Did you know that Jesus prays for us? That's right—the savior of the world, our Lord, prays for us. I don't know about you, but that makes me feel good.

"My prayer is not for them alone. I pray also for those who will believe in me through their message, that all of them may be one, Father, just as you are in me and I am in you."

John 17:20-21a

Those who believe through their message...who is Jesus talking about here? He is talking about us. We have received the message of Christ passed down all the way from the disciples, who made it possible for us to hear the word.

Sometimes we may not know what to pray, or we may feel overwhelmed. We can be confident in the fact that the one who loves us the most and knows us the best is lifting us up in prayer. I can't think of a better prayer partner.

What About Me?

Pray this with me:

Dear Jesus, thank you for praying for me. I trust that you always know what's best for my life, and are always working behind the scenes, even when I cannot see you. I'm so glad you are my prayer partner! Help me as I continue to learn more about you through prayer.

In Jesus' name, amen.

Day 86: Always With Us

I love packing for a trip. I almost like it more than going on the trip! I work hard to pack what I need, and I hate the feeling that I'm forgetting something. My family even makes fun of me sometimes because I'll start packing a week in advance of the trip. I can't help it!

As you go about your day, do you ever wonder if God is with you, or if he has forgotten about you? God isn't like that pair of socks or a hair straightener that you forgot to pack for a week at camp. He is *always* with us.

When you pray, you don't have to wonder if God is there or not. You can just start praying, knowing that God never left you. When you go to school, you don't have to wonder if God came with you. He did. When you are alone in your room, you're not really alone, because God is right there with you.

"No one will be able to stand against you all the days of your life. As I was with Moses, so I will be with you; I will never leave you nor forsake you."

Joshua 1:5

What about me?

Day 87: Psalm 23, Part 1

I love the psalms. No matter what kind of day I'm having, I can always find a verse to encourage me or correct me. They are made up of prayers and songs to the Lord that are still meaningful to us today.

One helpful thing we can do with our prayer time is to take a psalm and use it as a guide to pray through, and then using our own words to talk to God as well. Over the next few days, we are going to do just that. Psalm 23 contains many needs we regularly pray for, like protection, provision and comfort, so it's a great one to start with.

"The Lord is my shepherd, I lack nothing. He makes me lie down in green pastures, he leads me beside quiet waters, he refreshes my soul. He guides me along the right paths for his name's sake."

Psalm 23:1-3

What about me?

To pray in your own words:
Thank God for his perfect provision
Thank him for surrounding you with his peace
Ask him to guide your steps today and every day

Day 88: Psalm 23, Part 2

How did it go yesterday? Praying through a psalm is a little different than what you're used to maybe, but it's a good exercise to teach us new things about prayer. Let's dig into today's passage.

"Even though I walk through the darkest valley, I will fear no evil, for you are with me; your rod and your staff, they comfort me."

Psalm 23:4

What about me?

To pray in your own words:
Acknowledge that there will be hard times.
Thank God for his perfect protection through his presence in your life.
Thank him for his word, which comforts us.

Day 89: Psalm 23, Part 3

Today is the last part of Psalm 23, and God gives us some great promises in the closing verses. Read on!

"You prepare a table before me in the presence of my enemies. You anoint my head with oil; my cup overflows. Surely your goodness and love will follow me all the days of my life, and I will dwell in the house of the Lord forever."

Psalm 23:5-6

To pray in your own words:
Thank him for taking care of you, even when it looks scary all around.
Thank him for all his blessings. They are many.
Thank him for the grace and favor that surrounds you as a child of God.

You can do this with any Psalm that is special to you. This exercise will help you as you grow in your prayer life and learn to study the word on your own!

Day 90: Draw Near

In reading through old notes and journals as I wrote this book, I came across some notes from a sermon I heard in college. One phrase the pastor said really caught my attention.

He said that as children of God, we need to quit worrying that we are going to stress God out. I realized this was a fear of mine, and it wasn't something I just worried about in my relationship with God but in other relationships, too. It's not always successful, but I try really hard not to stress other people out.

It's good to not be overly dramatic (we girls can get that way sometimes) but to overly focus on not being dramatic can also be a burden. Sometimes worrying about not worrying others could be a hindrance in close relationships. Thankfully, we don't have to carry this worry into the presence of the Lord.

He has infinite resources and already loves us infinitely. Unlike us easily irritated humans, God isn't going to use up his last nerve.

We need to lay down the fear that we're going to stress God out. Instead, we need to learn to rest in Him! How freeing! We don't need another thought that holds us back from drawing deeply from our Savior to fulfill his purpose for our life.

Draw near to God. He won't be irritated.

"Let us then approach God's throne of grace with confidence, so that we may receive mercy and find grace to help us in our time of need."

Hebrews 4:16

What about me?

You Did It!

You did it, my friend! I'm so proud of you that you finished this book. It's OK if you missed some days here and there. (You can always go back and finish them later!) The point is you grew closer to God and have a stronger relationship with him. Just like that last verse we read in Hebrews, you should have confidence to come before the throne of God. That's what developing a good devotion time is all about: getting to know God, who is our savior, our shepherd, and our best friend.

It's about learning who we are in Christ and developing a healthy self-image and learning to control our emotions that can get a little wild sometimes!

And it's about learning how to memorize and apply God's word to our lives and talk to him through prayer. The lessons you've learned in here are so important. You'll carry them with you throughout the rest of your life.

Thank you for going along with me on this journey, and I'll talk to you again in Bloom Book 2, where we'll learn what God has to say about our friends and families. I can't wait!

Love, Samantha

A Note of Thanks

This book, like any book, would not be possible without the input, expertise, and support from a lot of people.

To Kurtis, thank you for believing in me (and among many things), acting as my IT and layout department, accountant, and showing me how to dream and cast a vision for the future. I love you.

To my Maloy and Hanni families, thank you for your constant support from the very beginning.

To my beta readers: Mom, Debbie, Hilary, Katie M., Mellissa W., Sarah S., Jessica A., and others. Thank you for your wise input and critiques.

Coming 2018:

Bloom Book 2

About the Author

SAMANTHA HANNI is the author of Change the Conversation and the Bloom devotional series. Her work has also appeared on Devotional Diva, To Love Honor and Vacuum, Families Alive and in the OCHEC Informer. From teaching dance classes to leading Sunday school and small groups, Samantha has taught and mentored students since 2007.

She graduated with a degree in journalism, and her passion is encouraging other people and seeing God's truth make a difference in their lives.

Samantha and her husband Kurtis live in Oklahoma City.

How to Connect with Samantha

Website: mrshanni.com
Instagram: samanthahanni
YouTube: Samantha Hanni
Facebook: Samantha Hanni Author

Made in the USA
Monee, IL
03 January 2020

19819556R00125